BRIDPORT PRIZE AI

EXTRACTS FROM THE NOVEL LONG LIST

JUDGE
Naomi Wood

redcliffe

First published in 2019 by Redcliffe Press Ltd
81g Pembroke Road, Bristol BS8 3EA

e: info@redcliffepress.co.uk
www.redcliffepress.co.uk
Follow us on Twitter @RedcliffePress

© the contributors

Follow The Bridport Prize:
Follow us on Twitter @BridportPrize
www.bridportprize.org.uk
www.facebook.com/bridportprize

ISBN 978-1-911408-60-4

British Library Cataloguing-in-Publication Data
A catalogue record for this book is available from the British Library

All rights reserved. Except for the purpose of review, no part of this book may be reproduced, stored in a retrieval system, or transmitted, in any form or by any means, electronic, mechanical, photocopying, recording or otherwise, without the prior permission of the publishers.

Typeset in 10.5pt Times

Typeset by Addison Print Ltd, Northampton
Printed by Hobbs the Printers Ltd, Totton

Contents

Introduction	5
Novel Award Partners	7
Judge's Report	9
While There Is Still Time Daniel Allen	11
7HZ Rebecca Blakkr	19
The Invisible World Hannah Colby	27
Brash and Frazil Órla Cronin	35
The Alchemy of Botany Kitty Edwards	44
The Well-Tempered Wife Leonora Gale	51
Leap of Faith Mel Gough	58
Dismember the Past Sean Gregory	64
The Other Son Aisha Hassan	72
The Good Steward Christopher Holt	79
Ghost Boy Emily Hughes	87
Seagull Pie Sandra Jensen RUNNER-UP	94
City of Blades George Kelly FIRST PRIZE	99
The Martyr's Hymn Wenyan Lu	107
The Only Life You Could Save John O'Donnell	116
Third Space Sophie O'Mahony HIGHLY COMMENDED	124
The Haven Sarah Reynolds HIGHLY COMMENDED	130
The Fleeting Sally Skinner	139
The Starlight Rooms Victoria Stewart	147
Looking for Romance (with Steve Davies) Ben Summers	153
Biographies	160

It's a long story

Writing a novel is like running a marathon, no matter what everyone tells you, it's best to go at your own pace. For those who cross the finish line, the next step is, now what?

That's where we come in. The Bridport Prize is the flagship of Dorset's Bridport Arts Centre and it began back in 1973. Almost fifty years later, it has grown into one of the most sought after writing prizes, attracting authors from across the globe.

In 2014, the Peggy Chapman-Andrews First Novel Award was established in honour of the Bridport Prize founder. It is run with commitment and in partnership with A.M. Heath Literary Agency, Tinder Press and The Literary Consultancy.

Beyond the prize

Our winning alumni include Kelleigh Greenberg-Jephcott's *Swan Song* published in 2018 and chosen as one of *The Times* books of the year then long-listed for the 2019 Women's Prize for Fiction.

In 2020, three of our winners will be published in the UK, US and the Commonwealth: Polly Crosby's *The Illustrated Child*, Deepa Anappara's *Djinn Patrol on the Purple Line* and Stephanie Scott's *All That's Left Of Me Is Yours*.

We are extremely proud of the part the Bridport Prize has played in discovering such innovative new writers. All our prize winners are proof that talent does indeed shine through. To the unknown writers who have a story to tell, please believe it could be you featured in these pages next year.

Enjoy the extracts. We loved them.

Novel Award Partners

The Bridport Prize is proud to work in partnership with the following organisations in the delivery of the Peggy Chapman-Andrews Award for a First Novel.

A.M. Heath Literary Agents
Founded in 1919 by Audrey Heath and Alice May Spinks, two women who challenged the conventions of publishing, we are a London literary agency still very much driven by a passion to help writers who want to shift, shape or enrich the wider cultural conversation, and provide irresistible entertainment.

Championing our clients' writing remains at the heart of what we do. As well as a century of experience, we bring energy, ambition, and a keen eye for detail to our work.

We're always looking out for original ideas combined with great quality writing, and we work with the Bridport Prize to encourage emerging writers. By helping to draw up the long-list and shortlist for the Peggy Chapman-Andrews Award for a First Novel, we aim to support the best new novelists to find publishers and readers across the world.

Website: www.amheath.com
Twitter: @EuanThorneycrof / @AMHeathLtd

Tinder Press
Tinder Press is an imprint of Headline, which in turn is a division of Hachette – one of the largest publishing groups in the UK. Tinder Press was launched in 2013, and is Headline's home for literary fiction, a space where classy, intelligent writing can thrive. Our stable of prize-winning and bestselling authors includes Maggie O'Farrell, Andrea Levy, Patrick Gale, Deborah Moggach, Chloe Benjamin and Guy Gunaratne. Last year our authors were selected for twenty prize listings in total, including the Costa, Women's Prize, Dylan Thomas, Man Booker, Goldsmiths, Jhalak and Wellcome.

Tinder Press prides itself on its bespoke approach to publishing, which starts with an editor's passion, which then galvanises the whole publishing house. Our authors are always at the heart of everything we do, and our aim is to nurture their writing and build careers that will endure.

Website: www.tinderpress.co.uk
Twitter: @Tinder Press / @maryanneharring

The Literary Consultancy
The Literary Consultancy is the UK's first and leading writing consultancy, offering editorial advice and manuscript assessment since 1996. Its aim is to provide honest, professional editorial feedback to writers to give them a better sense of whether and where their work might fit into the ever-changing market.

TLC and its team of world-class professional readers work with writers writing in English at all levels, across all genres. A popular 12-month mentoring programme, Chapter and Verse, supports writers to completion of a book project, alongside a suite of creative and practical events, and a yearly writing retreat, Literary Adventures.

The Literary Consultancy believes that fair, objective feedback can unlock the creative potential of writers at all levels, from emerging to professional. To achieve this, it focuses on cultivating the personal value of writing, equipping writers with the context, confidence, and skills they need to thrive and flourish.

Email: info@literaryconsultancy.co.uk
Website: literaryconsultancy.co.uk
Twitter: @TLCUK
Facebook: The Literary Consultancy

NAOMI WOOD

Judge's Report

I have to admit, the finalists of the Novel Category had to be separated from each other with a comb. On the last day of September, at the top of Hachette publishers overlooking the Thames, Mary-Anne, Aki, Euan and I had the tricky task of judging these novels excerpts on the criteria with which we judge any book: voice, style, characterisation, originality, narrative drive and polish. We also judged the first thirty thousand words on the invisible thirty that were to follow: on its promise. But all we really had to go on was what was on the page; each submission was entirely anonymous. I would like to share with you what we found most exciting about each novel excerpt.

First, *The Haven*, by Sarah Reynolds, which is Highly Commended in this year's category. Fifteen-year-old Emma Granger mysteriously sends a bunch of flowers to her parents, then promptly disappears. Twenty years later, Emma's best friend is still on the hunt to discover what happened to her best friend under such strange circumstances. Meanwhile, a girl has appeared in the Welsh mountains, with a possible connection to the cold case of Emma Granger. 'A memorably well written and often unexpected story of an unsolved disappearance, and its lasting effects on the lives of a family and a community,' commented Mary-Anne Harrington, publisher at Tinder Press.

The second Highly Commended winner is Sophie O'Mahony's *Third Space*, which follows Jenny Gallagher as she journeys to St Ives to find her father. Disruptive and disturbing, the narrative often shuttles between the trauma of the past and the hostility of the present, and it traces Jenny's breakdown in a Cornish cottage with humour, grace and tenderness. 'A haunting, claustrophobic glimpse into the disintegrating mind of a woman under immense pressure,' said judge Aki Schilz, from TLC. 'Written with real compassion, and a deft hand.'

Seagull Pie by Sandra Jensen is the Runner-Up of this year's competition. Breezy, witty, and very funny, the young narrator of this novel is a breath of fresh air as she recounts her family's haphazard life after being uprooted from South Africa to a dilapidated school-house in rural Ireland. The characters in *Seagull Pie* are eccentrically memorable: stone-deaf Bonma, a persevering but casually neglectful mother, and a young female protagonist who will make you smile at every turn of the page. Euan Thorneycroft, agent at AM Heath, commented: 'Charming and often laugh-out-loud funny, this is a deftly observed bildungsroman, the story of a young girl and her family attempting to start a new life in rural Ireland.'

And finally our winner: George Kelly's *City of Blades*. We were all unanimously gripped by this story of South London gangs, drug warfare and high-school romance, so much so that all of us felt very frustrated not knowing what was going to happen in the second half of this carefully scripted and structured novel. This is the *Wire* set in Croydon, and its lead detective is Deanté: a school-boy who is forced to investigate his sister's disappearance at the hands of two warring drug gangs. Fabulously written, expertly plotted, all of the judges agreed the novel was an absolute pleasure to read.

It was this submission which delivered most on all our criteria, and so, after two hours of back and forth, the *City of Blades* nicked it.

DANIEL ALLEN

While There Is Still Time

Synopsis
Billy Pockett is the youngest child of a rector in a country parish that fosters in Billy a love of the natural world.

Nature offers certainty. Other aspects of Billy's life test his understanding, with puzzles and secrets at every turn – the strange behaviour of his sister Charity, his father's faith, the curate's love life, his brother Jesse's banishment.

In response, Billy follows his own path, charting the life that flourishes in forests and marshes, nests and burrows. In doing so, he feels insulated from the capriciousness and peculiarities of his elders.

But Jesse's exile and Charity's decline into mental illness are family matters Billy cannot ignore. Part one ends with him wrestling with the dramatic implosion of his family.

In part two, Billy – Bill – is a middle-aged professor with a global reputation in climate crisis. Memories have faded. His parents are dead, Jesse too; and Charity has long been institutionalised, forgotten.

He encounters a young woman in three unrelated settings. Finally, she introduces herself and claims to be Charity's daughter.

Bill rejects her assertion: there was no daughter. But the woman is persuasive and asks for help in contacting Charity. Eventually, Bill agrees.

Charity's response when she encounters the woman confirms the two are indeed mother and daughter. Pregnancy and the pressure to give up her child caused Charity's descent into madness, and reunion prompts some restoration.

For Bill, aspects of his boyhood remain unexplained. Some secrets remain so. But reclaiming the sister he lost, and nurturing a love for a niece he never knew he had, allow him to live more peaceably in the present rather than dwelling on the shadows of the past.

Chapter one
Young Billy Pockett approached the corpse with a gnarly stave outstretched and dipped his head three times to the devil. 'Hex, vex and bob-bob-bob,' he said. 'And God bless Ma and Pa.'

The old dog fox lay on a pillow of dock and sorrel, the periwinkle sky shining in one blind eye. Pulled-back lips exposed the animal's teeth and suggested death and mirth had arrived together. Billy gave a tentative poke. Nothing.

He dropped to his haunches.

He heard a soft sigh then a buzz and saw the fox's flanks tremble minutely. And with a fizz the swarm erupted, ashy and metallic, a single mass in tight formation. It blasted upwards, pop from a bottle. It climbed and plummeted, dipped and darted, obscured the pinking sun.

Billy, startled, crabbed instinctively sideways and backwards as the insects raged. Unsteady on bent, reversing legs, he tripped on a tussock and came to rest in a furrow. Flat, motionless, awed, he watched through latticed fingers as the mob rampaged above his head and turned the heavens black.

Slowly the fury abated and in a minute the things were gone.

Billy sat up. The staff lay across his chest. He wafted it towards all points of the compass, laid it by his side and scrambled from the furrow. He approached the fox once more, careful this time not to waken it from the dead. Then he knelt and pulled a pencil stub and a scuffed red notebook from his pocket.

'*Fox*,' he scribbled, beneath the date. '*Dead in Woolmer's Acre. Infested.*' With greater care he wrote, '*Calliphora vomitoria.*' He looked over at the body then added, '*Buried with honours. R.I.P.*'

He stuffed the notebook and pencil back in his pocket and stooped to gather leaves. When he had an armful – goosefoot, good King Henry, bedstraw and flax – he stood over the fox and covered it carefully, a bright buttercup at its head and another at the tip of its rusty tail.

Billy rose and held still, head bowed, arms stiffly by his side.

'The fowl and the fox, all the works of thy fingers, the fish and the moon and the stars,' he whispered. 'And may it not be rabbit for tea.'

He stepped back and crossed himself.

'Amen.'

The old rectory was crying again. Whenever the mist rolled in, sometimes for days at a time, the damp buried itself deep in the cracked mortar and when there was room for no more it would ooze out again, white with pug and salt. On the upper walls, where ladders could hardly reach, moss grew thickly, and the slow meander of trickles and drips would turn it vivid. The weeping was pronounced whenever heat followed haar. On days like that – days like this – the old place steamed and blubbed. Visitors approaching the house by the gravelled driveway that divided round the neglected rose-bed, meeting again at the foot of the front steps, would see the upstairs windows with their rotting sills and streaky green tears and feel sad.

Jacques Adore the jackdaw clattered from a yew and landed softly on Billy's shoulder. The boy fed the bird a mint and ran a fond finger over its silvery neck. 'Kak-a-kak,' said Billy. 'Bugger and balls,' said Jacques, who also spoke Latin, and flew off.

Through a downstairs window, Billy could see his father standing at a table, poring over something. The Reverend Thomas Pockett had one arm and cartophilia. The arm he had lost in a war – *the* war, he called it – and the fondness for maps he had acquired in his youth. His own father, Walter Pockett, had been an explorer – Suffolk mainly, exclusively in fact – and had instilled in his son a sense of adventure which had endured until Thomas was five and a half and got lost alone in a small wood. Ever after Thomas had preferred pretend adventures. But with tumuli and contours, brooks, hamlets and henges laid out on paper and grid before him he would roam far and wide for hours and hours, savouring the rich smell of the imagined earth and drafting sermons in his head as he went.

The reverend reached for his cup of tea and with the shoulder of his missing arm nudged his spectacles further up his standing-stone nose, catching sight of Billy as he did so. He waved and congratulated himself for remembering quite quickly that this one was William.

'Fuck off,' said Jesse.

'I only asked,' said Billy.

'Well, don't,' said Jesse.

'But what is it?' said Billy. 'Tell me. Please.'

Jesse carried on rubbing the thing with a cloth.

'It's an ogre's bollock.'

Billy edged forwards. 'Where did you get it?'

'Off an ogre's bollock tree,' said Jesse. 'Now bugger off.'

Billy didn't move. As Jesse polished, there were glimpses of glass and brass.

'Is it a barometer?'

Jesse laughed. 'You flapdoodle. No, it's not a barometer.' He leaned back against the peeling whitewashed wall of the old stable, polishing still. 'Where have you been, anyway? Ma was looking for you.'

'I found a fox,' Billy said. 'Dead.'

'So?'

'It was all infested. *Calliphora vomitoria*. Millions.' He waved his arms over his head in imitation of a vast swarm.

'And what's that when it's at home?'

'Bluebottles, you flapdoodle.'

His brother snapped the polishing rag at Billy's face, stinging his chin.

'Ow,' said Billy.

'Well, don't be cheeky.'

Billy rubbed his smarting skin. 'Show me, Jesse, please. I won't tell.'

He knew instinctively that whatever Jesse was cleaning had been taken without permission. Not stolen, not quite, because Jesse often put things back when he grew tired of them. For now it was just borrowed.

Jesse came closer, the object still shrouded. Slowly he pulled the rag away.

'What's that?' said Billy. He was disappointed. It wasn't very interesting.

'Pressure gauge,' said Jesse. 'Worth a fortune.'

'Why?'

'Why what?'

'Why is it worth a fortune?' It didn't look to be worth anything. The glass was cracked and the casing tarnished and dented.

'Because, Billy Buttons …' Jesse held the thing before him, cupped reverentially in his two grimy hands. '… this here humble pressure gauge is off of …' He lowered his voice to a whisper '… the Tit-a-nick.'

'Oh,' said Billy. 'Well. What's that?'

'The Tit-a-nick. The ship, lubberwort. You mean you haven't heard of the Tit-a-nick?' Jesse gave a little snort. 'What do they teach you at that school?'

Billy considered. 'Nothing, really.'

'The Tit-a-nick – ' Jesse began.

A voice rang out across the yard.

'Jesse, is Billy with you? Your father says he saw him.'

Jesse ignored the voice and fixed Billy with a wide-eyed look. ' – was a huge ship, twice the size of Pa's church. Unsinkable, they said. But on its very first voyage it ran smack into an iceberg and sank to the bottom of the sea, ten miles down. Hundreds drowned and those what didn't were eaten by whales and polar bears and giant octopuses.'

Their mother called again. 'Jesse.' Louder, closer.

'You mean the Titanic?' Billy said.

He saw embarrassment flick across Jesse's face, come and gone quick as a rat.

'Correct, Billy Buttons. The Titanic. What I said.'

Flora Pockett, lean and strong, appeared in the doorway.

'Jesse, didn't you hear …'

She saw Billy.

'Where have you been, Billy? I was shouting myself hoarse.'

Billy opened his mouth to speak but his mother continued. 'I asked you to tidy your room. I've been asking you for days,' she said. Billy noticed her hands, chapped and raw on her slim hips. 'There are skulls and feathers and ... '

She stalled, uncertain of the collective noun for the bones and desiccated body parts, withering fungi, birds' nests, birds' wings, cows' horns, skeins of hedge-snared fleece, jars of pond water, dead bees in communion-wafer tins, flowers in presses, unusually shaped pebbles, mossy rocks, fossils, rusted tumours that might have been Roman jewellery, musket balls or bolts off a cart, and books on trees, galaxies, sea life, pond life and wildlife that clogged every surface in Billy's bedroom.

' ... stuff,' she managed finally.

'Oh,' said Billy. 'Yes. Sorry, Ma. I'll do it now.'

She stood aside to let him pass.

'I should hope so. He's on the six-thirty. Make sure you get it done by then.'

She turned to Jesse. 'You can stop smirking.'

'Not smirking, Ma,' said Jesse, smirking.

'What's that you're fiddling with?'

He looked down and seemed surprised to see the pressure gauge still in his hand. 'This? Oh, nothing much. Just, you know, something I found.'

'Found?' said Flora. 'Found where?'

Jesse lifted his head and looked evenly at his mother.

'On the beach, Ma, on the beach. Nothing to worry about.'

Billy skipped off across the yard. 'And don't let that blessed bird in the house,' his mother called.

*

Billy looked at the outstretched hand of the Reverend Robert Manley-Parker and marvelled at its cleanliness. It looked new, unused. Billy knew only the warty hams of country folk but this was a thing of purity and he hardly dared touch it.

'A pleasure to meet you, William,' said the Reverend, in a voice as rich as trifle.

Billy hesitated, then proffered a couple of shy fingers and the hand snatched them up, enveloped them and shook them heartily.

'Goodness me, you're the very spit of Dick, my brother's lad,' said Mr Manley-Parker. 'Though he's a head shorter and not as, well, swarthy, as you, William. Dick's always got his nose in a book, whereas I expect you're roaming the fields dawn till dusk.'

He let go Billy's hand and turned to Thomas Pockett. 'Marvellous countryside round these parts, sir,' he said, gesturing expansively. 'I'd never tire of it.'

Thomas nodded. 'Marvellous indeed.'

The children had been assembled in height order in the specially tidied drawing room whose malodorous damp patch above the piano was, luckily, in rare remission.

Mr Manley-Parker had descended graciously the line of junior Pocketts – the twins Jesse and Charity, Ruth then Billy – dispensing quips and pleasantries with only a hint of forced jollity.

He was a tall young man, wide with it, and looked to have been reared on butter and beef. He had a kindly face atop his clerical black, with rhubarb cheeks and hair of yellow rattle.

The position of curate had been vacant for some time. The previous incumbent had left to take on his own parish in the north country and Thomas had found him hard to replace, in part because he was particular. Two applicants had already been rejected because of, respectively, slurped tea and brown shoes. A third had withdrawn post-interview citing reservations over the liturgy. In reality, losing his wristwatch – case unproven but it was Jesse – and being liberally shat on by Jacques Adore had convinced the unfortunate priest that the Lord had other plans for him.

'Some interesting, ah, specimens in your room, William,' said Mr Manley-Parker from a point high above Billy's head. 'You're a collector, eh?'

Billy pondered. He wasn't. Not really. Things just attached themselves to him and were transported home where he would turn them in the light and try to divine their properties.

He was about to answer but Mr Manley-Parker got in first. 'Well, jolly good of you to give up your bed. I'm most grateful.'

He stretched out one of his unsullied hands and ruffled Billy's hair.

'Let's go and eat,' said Thomas.

When prospective curates visited, Thomas liked them to stay a night or two so he could assess the cut of their jib and their tea-drinking and footwear habits. But although the rectory was large, few of the bedrooms could be offered to guests because either they were full of junk and mice or were insufferably dank. Billy had no objection to sharing with Ruth on such occasions – they had midnight feasts and farted competitively – but he resented having to tidy his room. In his own mind, but by no objective measure, there was a kind of order to its chaos and he was reluctant to disturb it – insects here, mammals there; rock and iron on, beneath and round the table and sometimes in the bed. Nevertheless he had done what he could, stacking things neatly, pushing as much as possible into cupboards or battered trunks and stowing some of his more precious finds such as the sloughed skin of an adder and a fist-sized lump of glistening quartz in his secret place. He didn't want a stranger pawing them. After an hour's hard labour Billy had judged his work done and decided that the visiting minister would at least be able to navigate safe passage between the higher peaks of clutter.

At dinner that night – not rabbit but some indeterminate fowl – Thomas said grace and strapped on his fork. The fork was a wood and leather affair that he bound to the stump of his mostly absent left arm. An attachment of bent tin converted the fork into a rudimentary spoon as required. Thomas had designed the implement himself and although the fork had undergone many refinements since, it remained far from perfect and would frequently fall off if loaded with an overweight potato or even a posse of especially burly peas. But however impractical, the fork rendered Thomas nutritionally independent. Relying on others to carve up his food for him was an indignity he would do anything to avoid.

The rest of the family secretly detested the fork. When not in use, it loafed sinisterly on the sideboard, its hanging straps spotted with gravy, its tines darkened and notched by repeated incursions into Thomas's mouth. The ritualistic strapping-on of the fork delayed every meal such that the chief characteristics of Flora's cooking, which rose above functional only on Sundays, were lukewarm and congealed. And when the contraption detached itself during a meal, it was customary for everyone to down tools and wait while Thomas fixed it back in place, an awkward procedure that hastened the food's cooling and coagulation.

Straps tied and with a small nod and a quiet 'Thank you', Thomas signalled that eating could begin. Jesse, Ruth and Billy lowered their heads to their plates and swiftly shovelled in as much as they could in anticipation of a fork malfunction. Charity meanwhile nibbled elegantly on some vegetables – she didn't eat meat or indeed anything much – and manoeuvred others around her plate.

After a few obligatory compliments about the 'marvellous' food, Mr Manley-Parker turned to Charity and remarked on her hat. She often wore a hat indoors, for no reason other than she liked to. 'Charming,' he said, between mouthfuls. 'Did you make it yourself?'

It was a brave effort on his part but as disingenuous as his praise for Flora's cooking. Charity's hat was many things but charming was not among them. She delighted in selecting old ladies' clothes from church jumble sales and with a few deft pokes of her needle would unite and garnish them in unlikely ways. This particular ensemble was a simple thing in red felt. But on top of it Charity had erected, like the frame of a tent, the twin handles of a crocodile-skin handbag. From the handles hung glass beads and perforated painted bottle-tops suspended on gold thread. She looked like a bankrupt princess.

The other Pocketts were so accustomed to Charity's unconventional dress and adornments that none of them had even registered tonight's millinery.

Slowly she turned her pale green eyes to Mr Manley-Parker, sighed deeply and, after a considerable pause, said, 'Thank you. I did.' She offered him the makings of a sweet smile but suddenly switched her attention back to the pallid vegetables, nagging them with her knife, and appearing both melancholic and beautiful.

Mr Manley-Parker looked, in quick succession, confused, embarrassed and a little disappointed, but he ploughed on stoutly with an amusing anecdote about once nearly sitting on a bishop's mitre. 'I should add,' he said, touching the corners of his mouth with a napkin, 'that His Grace wasn't wearing it at the time.'

He leant back, anticipating at least a small ripple of laughter or, as had happened on previous occasions when he had told the same tale, some hearty guffaws. But the ensuing silence was broken only by the sound of cutlery and chewing – and a sudden crash as Thomas's fork fell off and hit his plate.

REBECCA BLAKKR

7HZ

Synopsis
7HZ is a psychological thriller set in London and Berlin, 2013. Oskar is a composer and bassist, stifled by the world of classical music and struggling with his masterpiece. He finds his muse in experimental musician Carnyx, who lures him into her dark world of sonic fetishism. When he hears recorded atrocities in her work, he realises his inspiration could also be his destruction.

At an underground club in Berlin, with his friend Leon, Oskar is captivated by experimental musician Carnyx. He follows her into a blacked-out sex room and breaks his hand, punching a security guard.

Losing his place in the orchestra, Oskar returns to London. His hand heals but then his bass is damaged when a gunshot sound triggers a stampede at a station. He finds documents hidden inside the bass, about sonic weapons and the deadly frequency 7HZ.

Unable to compose, he dreams of his dead twin sister Lenka. She was born deaf and he believes he stole her hearing. He discovers his elusive neighbour is Carnyx. Despite threats from her jealous brother Karl, they become lovers and she records his heartbeat during sex. Oskar starts to compose with the damaged bass.

Carnyx chokes her father to death, to capture the sound. She invites Oskar to a centenary concert of Stravinsky's 'Rite of Spring', where terrifying noises cause a riot. He suspects she orchestrated the station incident, but no one believes him.

In his warehouse apartment, Oskar thinks he can hear the frequency 7HZ. Karl arrives and attacks him, but falls down a lift shaft. Carnyx records his dying groans.

Oskar recovers and attends a performance by Carnyx, full of recorded atrocities. He burns his manuscript, then disappears.

After his apparent suicide, Leon discovers Oskar's new work, dedicated to Lenka. When performed, it has a profound effect on the audience.

1
F-sharp.

One terrible note, squealing in the dark. On and on and on like a drill in the molar. If it was broken up, he could find a pattern to it, a rhythm. He could place it somewhere. But this note was ruthless, singular. It didn't blink.

Behind the noise, he could hear someone. Footsteps, moving over floorboards, evenly spaced, calm. Too calm. Couldn't they see him, lying there? He wasn't sure if the darkness was in his head. There was pain somewhere in his body, but it was remote, a throbbing echo. The steps paused, right by him, thinking. Then came a dragging sound, something heavy coming towards him. The note was louder, sharper, pinning him to the floor.

It pierced his eardrum, a white-hot needle slowly inserting itself. Then it softened, became a worm, burrowing through soft tissue, winding down his cochlea. Even at the last defence, it didn't stop. It pushed on, advancing towards his brain, looking for a home to curl up in. He could feel it poking around, dislodging pictures, memories – a pig's mouth, frozen into a squeal; a flat green line stretched across a monitor; her pale eyes staring down at him.

Something was moving deep in his chest, the wild fluctuation of a trapped bird, wings thrashing against his ribs. Then it stopped. Its heartbeat flickering, slowing down to resignation. The note played on though, a relentless whistle skewering his insides. He was ready for it now, for a body no longer an instrument.

The pull of silence was irresistible.

11 JANUARY 1983 - 29 MAY 2013

He'd never heard anything like it. Not that there was anything to hear. There was nothing. Not even the sound of blood pumping around for company. The silence was absolute, inhuman, indifferent. It certainly wasn't golden. There were no choirs of angels, no *Requiem in D minor*. All that was left was a twisted kind of peace. Time to think.

He looked down at the man he was, the man he became. The scene seemed so absurd from above, like a religious allegory, full of symbols waiting to be decoded. The double bass was in the centre of the composition, flat on its back, stoically beautiful. Its Carpathian spruce was glowing in a shaft of light, straight from the hand of Rembrandt. He was next to it, of course. The Faithful Servant. He was on his back too, in a rather predictable shape. The perfect crime scene outline. His left leg was bent into something close to the recovery position, not that he'd be recovering any time soon. His right arm was bent, so his hand was ear level. He'd even got the Christ hand – two fingers raised, two curled down – like he was absolving someone.

He barely recognised himself with all that hair, that beard. Now he looked like some distant, uncouth relation. The clean-cut composer had been replaced by a wolf-man, an imposter. His features were the same, almost, under the swelling. He looked like his grandfather, with that high, stern brow and those green eyes. Not that he could see his eyes. One was just a purple slit, like a scored plum. The other was half open but bloodshot. With the tilt of his head, it appeared to be fixed on the bass. The Bohemian. It outlived him after all.

He watched the deep red pool creeping from the back of his head, the glossy coagulation. It was such a shame. He wasn't even that old. And that slack mouth, the bloody drool collecting in it. He was such a tight-lipped man, supposedly, yet he'd ended up with his mouth hanging open.

He spotted his mobile phone nearby, a mark of progress, advances in communication. It was probably switched off. His left hand was resting on the dreaded manuscript, strewn on the floor. At least the pages were covered in ink. The notes arrived after all. But they looked odd, like barbed wire.

Two figures were kneeling over him, dressed in green. One was holding his wrist, the other was lifting some kind of breathing apparatus from a bag. They were confident, methodical. And there was Leon, pacing around with his hands in that mop of hair. Perhaps he'd found him, or maybe it was a neighbour after all the noise.

Sound was returning. The soft hiss of a slow puncture. *Head trauma.* Fragments of voices. *Heart rate down.* He couldn't see himself anymore. It was black again. But he could hear. F-sharp. *What is that thing? Can you turn it off?* They dragged something away from him. The note stopped, ripped out at the root.

Can you hear me? A voice in his left ear, far away. He tried to turn his head and felt a tug of hair. His mouth tasted like iron. *Try to keep still.* A woman's voice. Milky white light in his eye.

He's going under. An ice-cold stream moving up his arm. A strange pattern in his breathing. *What's your name?* He could picture it, his name, like an open mouth.

'O – '

If he could speak it out loud, then he still existed. He could find her. Finish things once and for all. *We're going to help you breathe.* A mask was hovering over his face. He needed every last pocket of air in his throat.

'O – Oskar Ko – '

He screamed his name, but it came out faintly, a smudge of cloud in the night sky.

2

'Oskar Kokoszka.'

As he spoke it out loud, he could hear the familiar repetition. *Oskar Kokoszka Oskar Kokoszka.* He was stuck in a loop. The man before him blinked, two blinks, then three, processing the syllables of his name. It was always the same. His name caused some kind of cognitive disturbance. A brain-tangle.

When the man delivered his own name, it was short and weighty. A blunt instrument. It left Oskar with an empty head for a moment. Then he heard it again, in the distance. *Oskar Kokoszka Oskar Kokoszka Oskar Kokoszka.* A runaway train hurtling towards a precipice.

Oskar loathed pre-concert receptions. They were pre-tuned, pre-determined affairs where everyone revolved around the room, chiming out the same old exchanges. The concert would be even worse. He'd be playing the same old tunes, the ones that popped up at every fundraiser, symphonies that made his toes curl.

Another man swivelled into view, wafting in the smell of prawns and Pinot Noir.

'Johan Kropp. Chairman. Commerzbank.'

Oskar noted his phrasing, the implicit self-importance.

'Oskar Kokoszka, Principal Bass.'

There it was again, obediently exiting his mouth – his name, his profession – as though he had no say in the matter.

'Behind the Velvet Rope' had been devised by the new Corporate Relations Manager, Emilia. When Oskar saw the event on the orchestra website, he pictured a noose, made of plush fabric, dangling invitingly before his face. In Emilia's words, available in German and English, the evening promised 'an access-all-areas package, in which guests could experience a classical concert from the musicians' perspective.' So here he was, ready to be 'accessed'.

A sneer tugged at his insides. Welcome to my world, Herr Schmidt. Ask me anything, anything at all, as long as it's in English. Yes, the double bass is such a large instrument, not very practical on public transport. No Sir, I never tire of playing the *1812 Overture*. It's virtually my party piece now.

These events were a vital aspect of fundraising, according to Emilia. There were plenty of people who wanted a 'money-can't-buy' experience that cost a fortune. Car manufacturers, bankers, luxury hoteliers, they all wanted to feel the warm glow of association with a world-class orchestra. They didn't even call them Sponsors anymore, they were Partners now and he was expected to remember their names.

As he stood amongst them, like a memorial statue, he could feel a set of eyes on him. The dead, empty eyes of Robert Schumann. Only the composer's head and shoulders remained, poised on a nearby plinth. Oskar looked at his plump, pale features, the unmarked brow, the tiny cleft in his chin. His neck-tie was perfect, his jacket with barely a wrinkle. But there was something about his jaw, subtly receding into his neck in a kind of secret dread, that betrayed his future. This was pre-breakdown Schumann, before chronic pain furrowed his brow, before his career as a concert pianist was sabotaged by a hand injury, before he'd heard the term 'psychotic melancholia.' There was no glint of madness chipped into his eyeballs. The sculptor had left them smooth.

There were at least ten similar plinths around the room, with dead German composers teetering on top, devoid of pock-marks and flabby chins, hanging on to their chiselled swirls of hair. At the sight of them, empty-eyed in contemplation of their eternal silence, Oskar wanted to topple every plinth, one on top of the other. But instead, he stood there, slowly turning to stone.

He looked around at his friends, his colleagues. A couple of people from woodwind look mildly awkward, but in general no one seemed bothered by things at all; not in the same way as him. They all looked tanned and rested after the holidays, primed for the new season. He wondered if they'd noticed the dark circles under his eyes or the sallow complexion that came with being indoors all summer. Perhaps they'd spotted he was on his third glass of Riesling. It was hardly appropriate to be drinking so much before a performance, particularly for Principal, but he needed to forget about the manuscript. After weeks of agonising over it, with the deadline looming, it was a neat pile of nothing.

'Oskar Kokoszka, Principal Bass.'

Another introduction came and went. Oskar couldn't remember the man's name, nor which company he was from, something to do with petroleum perhaps. He looked much like the last guest. They were everywhere, grazing, grunting, content in their enclosure. This particular species, *Homo Superior*, had been trying to colonise classical music for years. At least they were all about to become cannon fodder for Tchaikovsky.

Another one pushed through, just as Oskar was biting into a miniature bratwurst. He was younger than the others, a prime specimen.

'Kasper Dix, BYK.'

'Os – k.'

A shred of meat was caught in his throat. Dix was staring, savouring the moment. When Oskar finally coughed up his name, the handshake that followed was somewhere between vice-like and paralysing. Another man joined them and Oskar tried to nod along to the conversation, occasionally raising an eyebrow at what he hoped was the right juncture. It was an effort when most of his brain, especially the part dedicated to panic and impulse, was consumed by the manuscript.

Another thought detonated in his head, flowering like a cluster bomb. The worst part wasn't even the pending humiliation – the performance to be cancelled, the failure to live up to his reputation, the news to be delivered to his parents – although that was bad enough. Far worse was the thought that his bass, The Bohemian, had finally given up on him. It wasn't a conduit anymore, it was back to being an instrument.

At first, he thought it was a temporary affliction. The notes had always been slippery, shy almost, but he'd hoped they were waiting for him in some dark, dusty recess. But after weeks of nothing, when they finally presented themselves, he was horrified. The notes were spewed out, like the bass was trying to rid itself of something. Transcribing them was impossible. Afterwards, when the bass had fallen silent again, he wondered if he'd been listening to its death throes.

He spotted Emilia across the room, ushering in another set of people, mostly men. They must have been Gold Patrons, possibly Diamonds. She certainly wouldn't be wasting her full smile if they were Bronze. Perhaps she'd taken them 'behind the scenes'. He pictured them all backstage, eyes tracking her neat, competent buttocks as she led them through a perilous world of unruly cables, scuffed walls and surly technicians. He preferred it on the wrong side of the proscenium, the dissonant feeling it gave him. It was like being on the reverse of a beautiful painting.

Emilia was smiling over now, moving through the guests in a sequence of short, precise angles that looked deceptively spontaneous. She was built for a show like this, with her engineered body and sleek, dark dress. As she slipped alongside him, he could tell she was still under the illusion he found her attractive.

'Klein,' she whispered, with mint-fresh breath. Emilia was gesturing to someone across the room. Oskar looked over to a pudgy little man, whose eyes were tracking a tray of canapés. He'd been briefed on him previously – big player in the art world, made his money in biotech, speaks five languages. No doubt some of Klein's money would be funding the schools' programme, so he should make an effort. But as he watched the man stuff another glazed delicacy into his mouth, the usual weary feeling returned. He drained the last of his wine and made his way over.

'Herr Klein! How are you enjoying the evening so far?' Klein was chewing it over. 'Oskar Kokoszka,' Oskar said, with extra emphasis. *Oskar Kokoszka Oskar Kokoszka*. He could hear it snagging in Klein's head.

'Like the artist?' he said, eventually. Perhaps a briefing on the market value of Expressionism was coming back to him. He was trying to catch the eye of a waiter, but Oskar blocked his view.

'Yes, a bit like the artist,' Oskar replied, 'although I believe he was Austrian.'

A platter of strudels hovered towards them, so Klein pincered one. As he shoved a pastry in his mouth, Oskar took the opportunity to go into unnecessary detail about the provenance of his name.

'My father was born in Prague, although Kokoszka's a Polish name. It's a different spelling and pronunciation to the Austrian name, the *sz* is softer. But it's my mother's fault really. The confusion I mean, with the artist. My father must have seemed quite exotic compared to English men, especially with that name. She was an art history graduate, you see. And when I was born, she couldn't resist calling me Oskar.'

Klein's mouth was hanging open slightly and Oskar could see a rim of wet crumbs along his bottom lip.

'Of course, the internet hadn't been invented then,' he continued, primed by alcohol. 'How could she know that years later I'd be disadvantaged in search engine results, forever the imposter.' He laughed a bit too long. Klein was about to excuse himself, but Oskar was just warming up.

'I've learned to embrace it now though. I can't deny it's a suitable name for a composer; the hints of Empire, it certainly evokes the virtuoso. And let's not forget, in the world of classical music, having an unpronounceable name is an advantage. It's not quite Dvořák, but it helps keep the riff-raff out.'

Klein looked relieved when Emilia appeared again, as though his nanny had brought him fresh underwear. Oskar watched her lead him away with a half-eaten strudel in his hand. He could imagine their conversation. Yes, of course, it's the best seat in the house. No, I'm afraid drinks are not allowed in the auditorium. It's certainly going to be a spine-tingling performance. Your spine will be tingled, Herr Klein. That's what you paid for.

Oskar grabbed a programme and headed to a nearby seat. As he flicked through the pages, he suddenly felt the blood drain out of him. There it was, towards the back – a half-page piece about his glittering career and the bass concerto he'd soon be premièring. The Artistic Director had confirmed it months ago, so of course it was in the programme.

He should have been ecstatic really, it was everything he'd worked towards. He'd won the scholarships, studied at the best institutions. He was right on cue. His heart sank even further when he saw the name of his concerto, *Winter Sleep*. It was only a working title, which now he hated, but there it was in black and white. He was committed.

The article also mentioned, in poorly concealed smugness, that the Gala would be featuring a commission for the first time in its history. This was big news, considering everyone was accustomed to the most important person – the composer – being dead. But Oskar was alive, almost, and soon his piece would be performed by one of the best orchestras in the world.

The man in the accompanying gold-toned image did look suitably convincing. Thick black hair was spilling on to his brow in pursuit of a myth-like status. He was wearing a slightly stoical expression, as though the burden of his role was heavy but not unbearable. A strange focal treatment had been used on him too, so his eyes looked sharper than the rest of his face and had a feverish quality. He'd seen this effect used on other Principal players, it seemed to invest them all with some kind of otherworldly expertise.

He didn't like the position of the bass either. The neck scroll was coiling around his head like a giant tentacle. Its presence reminded him of the honour it was for a double bass player to be chosen for a commission. They were seldom composers for some reason. Perhaps they got distracted by underpinning the greatness of others, or maybe they presumed people didn't like the low end of things. But none of it mattered if his bass was unwilling to participate.

He suddenly felt hot, so rushed to the cool air of the loading bay. As soon as he pushed through the door, a wave of nausea broke. He steadied himself against the wall, trying to catch his breath, then threw up behind a kettle drum. When he opened his eyes, he saw chunks of miniature bratwurst, splattered over his shiny shoes.

HANNAH COLBY

The Invisible World

Synopsis
The Invisible World *is a work of historical fiction, set in London in 1895 amidst the tumult of Italian anarchist activity. It tells the story of Elisabeth, an Anglo-Italian pianist, and the aristocratic Hedley St Clair, who brings Elisabeth into his household as tutor to his cousin, Hermione.*

Yet all is not as it seems. Hermione is the daughter of one of the St Clair siblings, but is it the aloof Edgar, the soldier, Lucien or the disillusioned priest, Francis? Or is it Hedley, living in sin with his paramour, Iona, or Hedley's sister, Bella? Elisabeth, however, has her own secrets. Her home is the centre of an anarchist circle and its leader, Giuseppe, is Elisabeth's lover.

To escape her feelings for Giuseppe, Elisabeth travels to the St Clair seat in Scotland, where she learns of the feud between the family and their relations, the Sinclairs. She meets Mhairie, a housemaid, and discovers hidden photographs of a woman, but when she ventures towards an abandoned cottage, she is assaulted. Afterwards, the attraction between Elisabeth and Hedley becomes physical.

Returning to London, Elisabeth performs at Iona's party, conquering a fear of public performance which is rooted in her own family tragedy. But Iona realises the attraction between Hedley and Elisabeth and dismisses her.

Elisabeth thwarts Giuseppe's attempt to bomb a theatre, but she is seen by another anarchist. Forced to flee London, she returns to Scotland where the mystery is solved by Mhairie. The woman in the photographs is Catriona Sinclair, a Scottish cousin who was raped by Lucien and who committed suicide after Hermione's birth.

Justice is served when Lucien is assassinated. The story concludes when Hedley joins Elisabeth in Scotland and informs her that the anarchist ring has been disbanded and it is safe for her to return home.

The Invisible World
1st Movement: *Allegro con moto, 4/4*
London, April 1895
1.
Elisabeth has decided to take this road because she doesn't want to smell the explosion.

She won't, of course. The breeze is from the north on this April afternoon but the warehouse where the bomb will be laid is far away to the south of the river. Yet she can still imagine the film of stinking green powder oozing upstream, like pondweed against the tide, through the slums of Westminster and down Dover Street to meet her. For Giuseppe has told her that this will be the biggest explosion to date, bigger even than the Observatory should have been last year. This morning, before she allowed him to kiss her goodbye, he had paced the floor around her, his fingers rigid with anticipation; at her gentle reminder that Bourdin had failed, he had merely curled the edge of his lip. 'But he was French, Lisetta. We are Italian. We shall do it better.'

Her blood, half-diluted by English sensibility, had not been roused by the assurance. She doesn't like to talk about such things over breakfast, especially with him, and she certainly doesn't want to know anything about the explosion if she can help it. Despite his promises that the only damage will be to the buildings nearby, she cannot shake away a persistent fear that someone may be too close when the bomb goes off. Admittedly, he hasn't failed her yet. But still she has chosen to take the longer route back from the west of the city to Leather Lane. It adds an extra mile to her journey but she doesn't mind.

There's another reason, in truth, for her decision to walk this way. Her shop is approaching, ahead and to her left, and there's an unconscious quickening of her step as she nears the window. It's a sunny day on this side of the city and the light is bouncing off the polished glass and straight into her eyes; it's impossible for her to read the gilt script above the door but she needs no words to tell her what's inside. As she assumes her usual position with her hands on the ledge before her and her nose almost touching the glass, the tension ebbs from her shoulders. Without thought, her fingers pulse a familiar pattern on the sill.

Minutes pass; maybe hours. The chimes of the great bell – G sharp, F sharp, E, B – pass unnoticed, as they always do when she stands in this place. Nothing can disturb her concentration. Yet if she would only draw her vision backwards, in stages, from the inside of the shop to her own wide eyes reflected in monochrome, and still further, to the street beyond, then she may well notice the advance of the man from behind her left shoulder. He's obviously someone who's used to attention, for only a dandy would match a mustard waistcoat to the ochre thread in the wool of his suit, but Elisabeth doesn't care a fig for the shine on his shoes, nor for the subtle check of his trousers. She's fixated on the objects beyond the glass, so close yet so far from her reach.

'Pianos?'

His voice is a cheerful tenor, confident but with a tremolo of surprise beneath it, as if the instruments are not what he expects to see. He isn't what Elisabeth expects to see either. Despite his polished appearance, his hat is slightly askew on his head, as if he's jammed it on in a hurry; beneath it, he's young, maybe five-and-twenty or so, only a few years older than her own age. He's a tall man, but she comes almost to his shoulder as he peers into the window and repeats again. 'Pianos?'

'Not just any pianos. That one is a Broadwood, there, and that one, in the corner, an Erard.' Quite unselfconsciously, never questioning his interest, she touches his arm to draw his focus into the deepest recess of the shop. 'And that one – there, you see? – that one is a Bechstein. That's the best make of piano you can find in London at the moment.'

'You sound like quite the expert.'

'I know a lot about pianos.'

The man shrugs, a quick lift of the shoulders. 'Well, I know nothing about pianos at all. I have to confess that I never even knew that there was a piano-shop here.'

'You mean you've never walked past it?'

'Never. My rooms are across the road on Albemarle Street. I have no cause to walk this way. I only noticed it because –'

'Because what?'

The man opens his mouth, shuts it again and examines the buttonholes of his cuffs intently. 'So why do you stop and look into this shop whenever you walk by?'

'Have you seen me before?'

'On occasion,' he replies. 'Were you listening to someone play?'

'No. I just wish that I was sitting there instead of standing here on the street.'

'I see. So you play yourself?'

'Since before I could walk,' she replies, as if such a statement is commonplace. 'My father is a musician. Do you?'

'No. My sister had tuition, but she was never very attentive. She's only good at things when she wants to be. I suppose she's probably forgotten anything she did learn now. She never used to practice.'

'You have to want to learn. Practice – playing – it shouldn't be a chore, but a desire. It should never be an effort, or you might as well not bother.'

The man is looking at her strangely. She knows why. It's because she doesn't speak like a London girl. She's seen that look many times before. There's an accent to her words that no one can place; it's just the slightest inflection, an extra weight on certain syllables that is recognised only as unfamiliar. People rarely ask her. She thinks that this man might.

'I quite agree,' he says at last. 'How often do you play?'

'I would play every day – every hour, and more – if I could.'

'Why don't you?'

She says nothing but looks down at her hands on the sill. Her fingers are not resting but arched upright and poised, ready, her forearms rigid with suppressed movement. She has unusually large hands for a woman, she knows. The sleeves of her dress are frayed a little at the edges and a stray thread has escaped down towards her wrist above her glove. The fabric is faded and unfashionably tight and the lace has been neatly darned with skill borne of necessity.

'You don't have a piano.'

The lift of her chin has merely a hint of defiance. 'Not any more.'

It is enough. Her wrist is so slender that his knuckles encircle the bones and overlap; she can feel the flyaway thread pressed against her skin. 'Come on. We're going inside.'

For only a second, she pulls back against him. 'Why?'

'I want to hear you play.'

The interior of the shop is sweetly musty with the scent of gas and beeswax. Elisabeth breathes it in and feels the sticky narcotic flow down her throat and into her blood. Her fingertips are tingling. They must cut a curious pair, she thinks, linked together, side by side; the man, roguish and flamboyant, with a glimmer of sunshine in his gold-woven clothes and the wrist of the dark-clothed girl held firmly in his grasp.

The shopkeeper is a stout man in a cheap suit and with a moustache that droops to one side. As they cross the threshold, he emerges from a murky corner in greeting and the two men move away at once to strike up a discussion. Elisabeth is left standing alone. To her right is an ancient cottage organ, one leg crooked and leaning inwards towards her, and she places one furtive palm against its side, pressing against it as if for comfort. The wood is as warm as her own skin beneath her touch.

A finger is crooked towards her, which she ignores. She's not in the habit of obeying instruction, and besides, she doesn't want to step into the centre of the room. It will leave her exposed on all sides. The corners of the stranger's mouth twitch; she has the distinct impression that her refusal to move forwards at his beckoning has amused him. Still unsure as to what this is all about, she watches him warily as he advances across the floor towards her. The shop is gloomy, despite the brightness of the sunshine outside – even in the better districts such as this, one eye must always look to economy, and it's a little too early yet to light the lamps – and in the half-light, he has a predatory air. He reminds her of the picture-postcards she has seen of hunting leopards: long and lithe, with a pale, yellow-flecked gaze that is fixed directly upon her as he draws closer. The shopkeeper trundles along in front of him, corpulent as a white-bibbed beetle. His cheeks are fairly shining with expectation. Unlike Elisabeth, he has assessed the cost of her companion's vestments with a single glance, and it's made him most happy to oblige.

'Madam. If you'd like to step this way?'

Stubbornly, she remains. 'May I ask why?'

Across the top of the shopkeeper's head, the amber eyes remain unblinking. 'I have explained to the gentleman that you would like to sample his merchandise.'

'I would?' Bewildered, she looks up at him. The feline illusion has vanished, and his face is alight with mischief. 'But I can't...'

'Of course you can.' It's a deliberate misinterpretation, and he turns once again to the shopkeeper, who is watching the exchange with smug indulgence. 'Can't she?'

'Of course.' One eyebrow arches as the shopkeeper glances from her dated costume to the taller man's impeccable checks, and Elisabeth feels herself bristle beneath the implication. 'Did you have a particular instrument in mind? We have a lovely Brinsmead which is quite astonishing in tone and quality and most suitable for,' – and just a hint of a pause –' a lady.'

This time, there is no moment of hesitation. In the face of such opportunity, all doubt and confusion is forgotten. From the moment she had first walked past the window, there had been only one that held her eye. 'I'd like to see the Bechstein.'

'An excellent choice.' The shopkeeper looks her over with new approbation. 'It's a beautiful specimen – barely used, I might add. The owner was most reluctant to part with it. It's as good as new.'

'I hope not. I've never enjoyed the sound of a new piano. I prefer something with a little history in its strings.'

'I'm sure you will find this most satisfactory. It was a much-loved family treasure. Do you play yourself? I am more than happy to provide a demonstration, if you wish.'

In response she pushes past him, her usual reserve forgotten in her impatience, and pulls the stool out from beneath the frame. Instantly he is behind her, fussing over her, smoothing the fall of her skirt as she takes her seat. She knows it's not for her benefit. 'Please, make yourself comfortable, madam. Do you require music?'

She shoots him a look that is almost pure scorn. 'No, thank you.'

Finger by finger, she loosens her gloves and drapes the discarded garments over her lap. The lid is open, and she traces one fingertip across the burnished frame, marvelling at the bloom of her own features in the satiny rosewood. In front of her, the keys glow with promise and as she settles her fingers across the ivory, she feels the familiar rush of memory, every nerve and tendon flexing with anticipation, as intimate as the touch of a lover. The air seems to thrum and vibrate around her. She is almost afraid to strike the first key.

From behind her, she hears his voice, strangely familiar now yet still muted by distance. 'What will you play?'

It's springtime, and she is in the company of strangers: the mood must be frivolous and bright. It should be carefree and fluent, undemanding for both performer and audience, yet pleasing to the ear. It should showcase her ability without flaunting her skill. Her mind skims through her repertoire, flicking over snippets of phrases and melodies. What to play?

She knows, of course, the melody that she cannot play. It is the first that comes to her, and always is, every time she sees the keys ranged blankly in front of her. As she stirs into wakefulness each morning, and as she drifts into sleep every night, it is there, in the back of her thoughts; at every moment, in the rippling laugh of a child or a single note of a street-musician's song; it is there within her, always, heard within but never aloud.

With effort, she shakes it away from her. 'Oh, I don't know. I'll think of something.'

In the end, the decision is easy. Effortlessly her right hand picks out the opening bars of a Mozart sonata, a simple yet delicate composition, and one which she has known by rote since childhood. As her fingers skip across the notes, she looks to the window and allows herself a moment to examine the reflection of the man behind her, sketched like a chalk outline upon the panes of polished glass. He is watching her, she knows. She can feel his eyes against the seam at the back of her dress and on the sweep of hair at the nape of her neck, as thick and glossy as tar, where her head bends towards the keys. Maybe it's a trick of the light, but the hint of a smile seems to have disappeared from his expression.

As the final tremolo fades into silence, there's a polite smatter of applause from the shopkeeper. 'Bravo! That was excellent. A faultless rendition, if I do say so myself.'

Elisabeth ignores him. Her attention is still fixed on the man who brought her here. He is watching her intently, his eyes slightly narrowed. A dismissive shrug sums up his response. 'Pleasant enough, I suppose, but not for a girl who has been staring at these pianos for a fortnight or more. Won't you play something a little more challenging?'

Beneath his words is the thud of the gauntlet falling to the floor, and temptation rears up within her before she can hold it back. 'But of course.'

Considerations about the climate, season and company are forgotten; such provocation calls for something more Prussian by nature. Schubert escapes from her, almost without thought, and the rousing crescendo of the march builds to press against the confines of the shop, the notes pushing against the mortar with enough force to break the bricks. The air is so thick and claustrophobic with the swell of the music that with her every exhalation, a flurry of semiquavers erupts on frantic breath. She urges herself on, allegro, finishing the phrase before the room can collapse in on her, and finishes with a final triumphant flourish, allowing the last chord to resonate through her before she lifts her fingers from the keys. Smoothing her expression into one of deliberate nonchalance, she swivels on her stool to face him, her eyes belying her triumph; but to her intense irritation, he has his back to her and is nose-to-forehead across the counter with the obsequious shopkeeper. He does not appear to have noticed the music at all.

Biting back her frustration, she strains to catch the tail-end of their conversation. He has his hands shoved deep in his pockets and is leaning forward in concentration. 'So you would recommend a German model?'

'Without question. Our English manufacturers are good, of course. Your everyday listener may not know the difference, and an average musician can make a remarkable instrument sound very normal indeed. But for the discerning audience, such as yourself, there is something that sets the Bechstein apart. It's the German mark of quality, you see. I can only imagine that over the next twenty years, it will be the ambition of those at all levels of society to have a German-crafted piano placed in the drawing-room.'

'That's very interesting. I must tell you that I'm not looking to purchase – not yet. But I do have a business proposition for you. This good lady,' and he turns and gestures to Elisabeth, who jumps in consternation at being caught eavesdropping and almost forgets her growing disbelief, 'this good lady is in need of a place to play a piano. I would like to hear her play, and there can be no doubt that the sound of music will bring curious customers to your door. Am I correct?'

'You are, sir.'

For once, the words of both her native tongues desert her.

'I would like to pay you, my man, a sum to be negotiated, which will allow this lady to come into your shop at this time each day and play for – how long – an hour? Is that enough?' Without caring for the answer, he continues. 'In return, you must provide refreshment, open windows and any instrument of her choice. Is this an agreeable proposition?'

'Most agreeable,' the shopkeeper murmurs and Elisabeth sees that his expression – strained at the eyebrows, gaping at the jaw – exactly matches her own. 'Do you have a rate for this service in mind?'

'Of course. Pass me that pen, will you?' He scribbles something briskly on a scrap of paper and pushes it back across the counter. 'Will that suffice?'

'Very well, sir.' A nervous flash of a lizardlike tongue and new moisture glistens on the shopkeeper's plump pink lips. 'Very well indeed.'

'Excellent. We can start tomorrow. Does that suit you?' The last question is directed towards Elisabeth, as if he has belatedly realised that she might have a part to play in the conversation. 'Do you have any further requirements?'

ÓRLA CRONIN

Brash and Frazil

Synopsis
We inscribe our desires on Antarctica. The novel Brash and Frazil, *a commercial-literary crossover, explores this wilderness owned by no-one and everyone. It follows Grace, a scientist and sailor, as she tries to protect her birthplace.*

Grace has written a scathing environmental impact assessment of a proposed hotel, recommending it shouldn't be built. The proposed site is a decommissioned research station in Antarctica. The ripples from a report she has written gather into a wave which threatens to engulf her career, her relationships and her integrity.

She takes a holiday to help run a sailing expedition in Antarctica. On the trip she meets Yann, a Belarusian engineer. They become lovers.

On returning home, Grace is offered a lucrative job by Yulia, the Belarusian entrepreneur behind the hotel development. The job comes with one condition: that Grace rescinds her report. She rejects the offer, and flies to Belarus to spend time with Yann.

While in Minsk, Grace is summoned to meet the Minister for Natural Resources, who asks her to modify her report. She is shocked to discover that he has a strange lever: her parents received a bounty to give birth to her in Chagall, the Belarusian Antarctic Research Station. If the arrangement founders – if, for example, Grace brings the country into disrepute, the gift converts to a debt.

Grace is torn between maintaining her professional integrity and protecting her father's business from the Faustian pact he's made. The pressure increases when Yann is arrested and imprisoned.

The campaign for Yann's freedom culminates in a city-wide flashmob. Yann is released, but he ends his relationship with Grace. The Antarctic Treaty Consultative Committee rules against the hotel. Grace is relieved, but realises that the scramble for ownership of Antarctica is only just beginning.

Brash and Frazil
Chapter 1
Ciara opened the throttle. She looked back towards *Jinkiri*, where Doug was waving from the foredeck. Her wake carved a pleasing parabola on the glassy sea behind the rubber dinghy. She slalomed around metre-high

growlers. The hull rose onto its own wave. She hunkered forward, using her bodyweight to keep the boat level. Bergy bits around her glistened in the sunlight. A mile away, cliffs soared from the rocky beach. Névé dribbled from the ends of glaciers. She cut the engine. In the stillness, she could hear frazil ice hissing and popping, and the distant craaking of the penguin colony on the beach. Uncouth brown skuas shrieked above her, ready to dive-bomb anything resembling food.

She drifted towards a berg chiselled to resemble Hepworth's Fugue II. Antarctica is one vast Rorschach test. Every season, expedition clients on *Jinkiri* vied with each other to find esoteric similes for the icebergs honed by wind and sea. The artists spotted Anish Kapoor sculptures. The architecturally inclined saw the Guggenheim Bilbao. The less culturally competitive saw Minecraft palaces.

She sometimes winced at the clients' murmured 'awesomes' and 'incredibles' while they patted down the beauty into bite-sized photos. Orcas were always 'cute and cuddly', even when they were tearing an emperor penguin apart in a frenzy of blood and feathers. But she still laughed at slapstick penguins strutting like the Three Stooges. Beginner's mind seemed impossible to maintain.

She had been lolling for long enough, and had no wish to encounter three metres of grinning, hungry leopard seal. The grey dinghy could be mistaken for a juicy meal, and leopard seals swam much faster than her little outboard could drive. Doug might be watching her progress through binoculars from *Jinkiri*'s deck. They would usually have gone ashore together, each in a separate dinghy for safety, but Doug had stayed for a telcon with one of next season's expedition leaders.

She started the engine, giving it enough power to maintain steerage, slowing down so that the grease ice near the shore didn't damage the hull.

The portable radio crackled. 'Chagall Station to *Jinkiri* mobile,' crooned a mellifluous Russian accent.

'*Jinkiri* mobile, over.'

'Hello, Ciara. What's your ETA?'

'I'll be at the beach in a few minutes.'

'Ah, great. The kettle's on. See you there.'

'Thanks, Michail. *Jinkiri* mobile out.'

Michail was bulky in his red down-padded survival suit. He was striding towards a patch of beach which was reasonably clear of boulders and penguins.

'*Privet*, Ciara! It's so good to see you,' he yelled.

She stopped the engine and canted the heavy propeller clear of the water. The dinghy skittered onto the black sand. Michail grabbed the line she threw, and hauled. She hopped out, careful not to splash icy water into her seaboots. Together they dragged the boat up several metres beyond the waterline and tied it to a large, guano-smeared boulder. There were no tides here, but a little tsunami from a collapsing iceberg could wash the dinghy off the beach.

Ciara and Michail held each other in a long, belly to belly hug. Michail had been on a field trip last time she'd visited, so they hadn't seen each other for a year. He was her closest friend among the twenty staff of Chagall Station. He'd overwintered five times, and was renowned for his prodigious capacity for vodka, his ability to decode weather, ice and microbiological samples, and his rare but fiery tirades about 'politikers' and 'tourits'. He looked the part of a true Antarctican, with a luscious, hoary beard, leathered skin and clear blue eyes narrowed against the glare of sun on sea and ice. Exchange the red survival suit for a canvas smock and he'd pass for one of the early 20th century explorers.

'Hey, *mlodšaja siastra*, how are you these days?'

She found being called 'little sister' heartwarming. She usually called him whatever polyglot endearment popped into her head, or just '*mo chara dhil*', my dear friend. They'd managed to navigate beyond the clumsy pass he'd made at her one New Year's Eve three years ago, transmuting alcohol-induced lust into a deep and easy companionship.

'And you remembered our angle grinder. I know you love power tools. I wasn't convinced we'd ever see it again.'

She smiled. 'It's been great, thanks. Saved us a day of hacksawing through a stupid jubilee clip.'

Michail heaved the equipment onto his shoulder. Normal neighbours further north handed a jug of milk or a cup of sugar over the fence to those caught short next door. Within the Antarctic Circle, equipment, spare parts, books, medicine, charts and delicacies diffused through the sparse but convivial network of scientists, base support staff and sailors. Some items – like the jars of homemade mincemeat from Palmer Station – circulated forever, a circumpolar current of unwanted gifts. But these were only flotsam compared with the deeper tides of goodwill and favours that bound the strange community together. Last season, Ciara and Doug had spent two days tacking into a fierce south-westerly to transport a Belarusian scientist down the Peninsula to Port Lockroy. A hernia, combined with a suspected blood clot, meant that he couldn't be flown from the airstrip on King George's Island; hitch-hiking a cruise ship headed to South America was his best chance of specialist treatment. This favour rendered Ciara and Doug part of the family at Chagall Station, the home of the Belarusian Antarctic Program. They'd eaten endless steaming bowls of borscht there, and were always plied with tarry coffee, honeyed pastries and copious vodka.

As they walked towards the station, Adelie penguins – and the occasional interloping chinstrap – skittered out of the way. Ciara knew that if she stood still, her seaboots would be thoroughly investigated by inquisitive beaks. Most of the young ones were self-sufficient now; a few bedraggled late developers huddled, noisy and grumpy as human teenagers.

The base was plonked behind a rocky outcrop. Though Chagall Station was named after Belarus' most renowned purveyor of mesmerising colour, it was a drab, unprepossessing collection of aluminium clad shipping containers. Ciara and Michail picked their way through boulders until they reached the main cinder path leading from the garages and warehouses to the main building. Several minutes' trudging brought them through the double insulating doors into the fug of the recreation block.

Ciara was bemused by the size of the crowd milling around in the disrobing area. The entire summer station staff – twenty or so burly men – had turned up, all intent on enveloping her in bear hugs.

Once she'd shed her bulky outdoor clothes and been fitted with a pair of felt slippers, she was bustled into the main living area. In front of a coffee pot and a steaming samovar sat a plate of kataifi pastry, resembling pale shredded wheat, arranged in the shape of a nest. Beside it, leaning against the samovar, was a foot-high painted cardboard cut-out of... a heron? A flamingo? It tilted over the cake, almost dipping its beak in the honey and walnut filling.

Aleksey, the cook, elbowed his way to the front of the welcoming party.

'We heard you had a ... I think in English you say "bun in the oven"? Well, we decided to make you a nest, in honour of the real stork which will find its way to you in a few months.' He gestured towards the wonky bird.

Ciara, though disconcerted by the streaking speed of gossip, laughed along with the applauding men. Her news was always going to be common knowledge eventually. A female sailor was already a rarity in these latitudes, and a pregnant one was definitely gossip-worthy, especially at the end of season when the scuttlebutt was thin. Ciara noticed that after the initial flurry of congratulations, no-one asked her a single question about the baby, including the obvious one: how were they going to manage their little household, given that their home and business was a seventy-foot yacht?

Ruslan, the station commander, was beside her.

'Stay for dinner, Ciara. We'll make up the guest-room.'

Ciara and Doug were rarely more than an arm's length from each other. They hadn't spent a night apart since their season began, back in November. She figured he'd grouse about her banqueting without him, and he would be deeply jealous of her having her first bath in four months, but these days, he was still so dazed with joy at idea of the Minnow, he indulged her every whim.

***

'Doug, if the Minnow's a girl, I'd like Gráinne. Or Grace, to save endless mispronounciations.'

Doug smiled. 'Grace O'Malley, pirate queen, or Grace Darling, lighthouse keeper?'

'Both.'

'Sounds good to me.'

* * *

She radioed from the comms office.

'You're telling me that you're being held hostage with hot meals, a wood burner and a cosy bed?' said Doug, the radio rasping his sentences.

She'd been getting cabin fever for the past couple of weeks. They'd dropped off their last clients of the season, a camera crew, at Port Lockroy, where they would finish their film and join a cruise ship to travel home. Doug and Ciara were on their way back to Ushuaia. They were facing into a gruelling week of sailing north, 'uphill' across the savage Drake Passage. King George's Island, where Chagall Station co-existed with a smattering of other research stations and an airstrip, was the last landfall between the Antarctic Peninsula and the gnashing Southern Ocean. She knew he didn't begrudge her a night off.

'You'll be the last guest of the season. They'll treat you like a queen.'

'Yep. That's what I'm banking on. No vodka for me, though.'

'Ha! *Kvass*! A hefty dose of that vile bread beer! That's your penance for partying without me.'

* * *

After dinner, people drifted off in ones and twos, leaving only Ruslan and Petr, the medic, at her table.

'We have a proposal for you, Ciara.'

* * *

Jinkiri's black hull gleamed in the sunlight. Doug was smiling as he secured her line.

'No boarding until you hand over the goodies.'

She handed him the drybag and heaved herself up over the rail.

'Miss me?' She moued.

'It was very peaceful around here. Dull, too. Can't wait to hear about your night on the tiles.'

He nuzzled her lips, and squeezed her shoulder.

By the time she'd degombled – brushed off stray ice and sand, and stripped off the unwieldy layers – mittens, seaboots, bobble hat, scarf, balaclava, survival suit and thermal 'romper suit' – the kettle was whistling, and he'd found Aleksey's *kartoshka*. It was too late in the season for Doug to call her a 'degombled womble': in-jokes wear thin after a few months. They sat at right angles in the doghouse, munching their pastries and drinking tea.

'So...?'

'It was...interesting.'

'That doesn't sound as though ye were dancing on the tables. What's new?'

She talked slowly at first, and then more hurriedly. He stiffened, his face reddening as his expression chilled.

He was always the careful one. That had kept them safe over the years, but it had also kept them weatherbound in dreary harbours when, with some gumption, they could have been skimming along under deep-reefed sails and a storm jib. She'd predicted Doug would be sceptical. He would always be in a no-change, low-risk corner and she was usually propelled by radiant visions of what might be possible. But his cold anger was unfamiliar.

On and on they wrangled. She found that somewhere between the beach and their anchorage, she had decided to accept Ruslan's offer. They had two days to respond, before they needed to depart for their usual off-season berth on the rickety pier in Ushuaia. By the end of the first day, she was exhausted. She had wheedled, cajoled, wept, and threatened but Doug was implacable. There was something visceral in his resistance, something beyond logic. She took him through the information pack.

'Petr's a qualified obstetrician. We'd never be able to afford someone like him.'

She pointed out that Petr had worked in Burkina Faso in rural clinics, that he was used to minimal equipment and support.

'There's the telemedicine service...'

'And if something goes wrong? I know in your fantasy world nothing ever does, but...'

She waved the flight schedule for August: summer flights would start a month before she was due, so if things weren't going smoothly, she could fly out then.

They spent next day on chores, lost in their own thoughts. Periodically one of them would find an argument or a counter argument. They dug themselves deeper into their respective holes. For Ciara, the proposal had exposed the faultlines in their future. She remembered her grandmother saying that a body needs somewhere they can retreat to in any kind of storm, both the real ones and those in their heads. War-time nursing 'across the Water' in London had convinced Nana that even if you claimed the world as your home, you needed a tiny patch to sit down on. Though Ciara could barely admit it to herself, she had started to long for a hearth and stool of her own. Their boat gypsy life was starting to feel as creaky as her joints.

Doug was servicing the mainsail. It could have waited until they returned to Ushuaia for winter refit, but he loved wielding the sailmaker's palm, the clever leather sling reinforced with a penny at the base of the thumb to force the needle through stiff canvas. Stitching sails connected him to centuries of sailors, and the precise, repetitive motions gave him time to reflect.

She sat down beside him. He moved up the coachroof, leaving a studied distance between them.

'Doug...'

He interrupted. 'I thought we had a plan, Ciara?'

'Yes, I guess we did... do.'

She rushed on to cover up the giveaway tense. 'But this offer lets us move straight to the big plan. We could move straight to Ireland.'

'Oh, so it's green, green grass and a dreich drizzle you're after?'

'There's no need to be vicious. Minnow would have a doting Nana and Grandad. It'd have cousins...'

And, she thought, a child bred and buttered there wouldn't stumble over 'Stephen's, err, Boxing Day', but would know it was Wran Day, would know that if someone was described as *flaithiúl*, their generosity was suspect. Would know that grand didn't mean posh.

'You could build boats. I could finish my PhD. We don't need to put the future on the long finger anymore'. Again, the giveaway tense.

'You said you wanted to set up an expedition management business. We agreed Ushuaia would be the perfect place to do that. You said you were okay with me carrying on sailing. Did you have your fucking fingers crossed behind your back the whole time, Ciara?'

'I'm not trying to make a fool out of you, Doug. We were going to make it all work, of course we were. But why would we hang onto a bodge that made the best of a shitty situation when they're offering us our dreams on a platter?'

He thumped the deck with his leathered fist. Leaden dread crawled through Ciara.

'I wanted to be the one to hand you our dreams on a platter, Ciara. It might have taken a bit longer, but clean, hard work would get us there too. It doesn't feel shitty to me at all. It feels real. And worthwhile.' There was a tremor in his voice.

He fiddled with the leather palm, clicking the popper open and closed and open and closed. His fury seemed to have abated.

'This isn't like winning a lottery. There'll be consequences.'

They went to bed exhausted and contorted with disappointment in each other. They lay back to back, not touching – quite a feat in their narrow bunk. As sleep sucked them down, their rigid bodies relaxed and curled up into two commas. Finally, drowsing, they cleaved together and fucked, clawing past the anger and hurt to find each other. The last thing she heard as she drifted to sleep was Doug murmuring.

'We'll figure it out, my love.'

They stayed in bed in the morning drinking coffee, their skin sleepsoft, their legs entwined. Doug was melting. Their connection had gentled his fears to the surface.

'I do want to be around for it, her, him, I do. I could still sail the season, though. The Minnow wouldn't be any better off with me there twentyfour seven. Look at my Dad. He didn't spend a single night away from home, but it's taken me years to get over his endless carping.'

'You won't be like that. You'll cherish them, and nourish them. I want you to be there for it all, the walking and the talking and the first day at school. And if you aren't there, who's going to teach them to wolf-whistle, how to find the constellations, how to change a starter motor? Who's going to nag them to screw the lid back on the marmalade? Who's going to read Bear Hunt to them with all the actions and sound effects? And I can never remember the last verse of the Spaghetti Song…'

His smile was watery. He had been so staunch and sensible when she had shown him the line on the test stick. But now tears were blurring his brown eyes, and he clenched her hand.

She realised that they were now coasting towards the decision.

'We'd be able to buy those winches you slavered over.'

'Oh, new winches? You know where my soft spot is, alright…'

She wrapped her arms around him. 'It's the next phase of the adventure, my sweet one.'

He stroked her hair, and sighed.

She picked up the radio handset. 'Chagall Station, this is *Jinkiri*, over.'

Petr answered immediately.

'Go ahead, Ciara.'

'We'll do it, Petr. Over.'

'Affirmative, Ciara. I copy "we'll do it."'

She could hear Petr's delight, even filtered through the formality of radio-ese.

'So, Ciara, your child will be a member of a very exclusive club. The 12th citizen of Antarctica. Chagall, out.'

KITTY EDWARDS

The Alchemy of Botany

Synopsis
The Alchemy of Botany *is a novel about the magic of science. Myopic botanist, Gill Pearce, is studying the role of colour in medicinal plants. When she discovers the existence of a blue flower that can heal all illnesses of the mind, she travels from London to Nepal. There, she must decide whether to stick to her scientific training or follow her instinct to find the flower as well as the secrets of her own heritage. This is a modern day adventure and romance.*

Dr Gill Pearce grew up believing in magic. This belief was encouraged by her mother Anya, who is descended from a Himalayan people known for their deep affinity with plants. Anya used to work for the pharmaceutical company Phoenix. She was fired when she disagreed with their synthetic mass production of herbal medicine. Her subsequent breakdown led to Gill's resolution never to believe in magic again.

When Gill receives an unusual herb from Phoenix, she finds herself remembering her childhood. Unaware of Phoenix's involvement in Anya's past, she accepts their offer to fund her research. In the Herbarium where she works, Gill discovers old reports of a Himalayan blue poppy said to heal the mind. She realises this is the magical blue flower Anya had spent her life looking for.

Phoenix send Gill to Nepal to find the poppy. There, she discovers that Anya's breakdown was caused by medicine that Phoenix tested on her during a drug trial. Only the poppy can now heal Anya's mind. Gill resolves not to help Phoenix but they are trailing her. She is saved from their attack by an avalanche but the poppy is destroyed.

Back in London, Gill discovers ancient seeds from the poppy in the Herbarium. The final magic is her belief that she can grow them.

To see a World in a Grain of Sand
And a Heaven in a Wild Flower
Hold Infinity in the palm of your hand
And Eternity in an hour

Auguries of Innocence
BY WILLIAM BLAKE

Origin of 'Science' - "from Latin *scientia* knowledge, from *sciens* ... , present participle of *scire* **to know**..."
[Chambers Dictionary of Etymology, emphasis added]

BEGINNINGS
Twenty years ago – Summer
The child lay on her belly in the grass, running her fingers along the smooth green stems. The colour was vibrant against the black shadows and the dark soil beneath. Delicate veins ran in mesmerising lines from the tip to base of each blade. All around her tiny white daisies tilted their heads upwards, following the sun across the sky. From East to West, as they did every day.

So perfect, she thought. This was her world, and it was magical.

She rolled onto her back and stared up at the blue expanse above her. It reflected on the water of the river that ran by her side. Filling her mind and flooding her with happiness. Blue was her mother's favourite colour, and Gill thought it might be hers too.

Her mother wasn't happy, not all the time, Gill knew that. No one was. But there were some days when her mother's mind got stuck, in a wasteland without colour or light. Gill could see it in her eyes, feel it in her touch.

On the good days they searched for something that would help, a panacea. Her mother knew about plants and how they could heal. Ground into paste or drunk as tea. So they scoured the verges and woods, hunting down seeds and cuttings, looking for one plant in particular. A flower, in the exact same colour as the sky.

'Just imagine,' Gill's mother would say, closing her eyes and touching the centre of her forehead. 'A flower that holds all the joy of heaven.'

One day, Gill promised herself, she would find that flower for her mother. She would do anything it took. Cross oceans and mountains, barefoot if she had to. Learn the name of every plant in the world and examine them all.

Then her mother would never again go to that place where Gill was scared to follow. And they could live together forever, happily ever after.

With these plants, beneath this sky. And their world need never change.

CHAPTER 1 – MELISSA
London, Friday 18 January
Dr Gillian Pearce peered into the microscope, one hand resting on the ribbed metal of the focussing wheel and the other clutching a pencil hovering over a half-drawn sketch. Her jaw was set and her features calm, her breathing slow and steady. Beneath the lens, a hidden world unfolded. Lost in ridges and bumps, shadows and light, the cross section of the herb revealed its secrets to her under the intense magnification.

The individual box-like and hexagonal cells seemed to pulsate against each other, their patterns repeating over and over again with a hypnotic call. She knew they couldn't be pulsating, not really. It was a nice idea, but it was impossible. Plant cells were fixed, a tough cell wall surrounding the membrane. It must be an effect of the light shifting through the water she'd placed on the microscope slide, tricking her brain.

There was a time, many years ago, when Gill would've believed there was something magical about what she saw down the lens. But not anymore. She'd learnt long ago to grab such flimsy thoughts by their wings and shove them into a box, before they took control. Gill knew better than most people how dangerous it could be, to blur the line between fact and fantasy. Even so, her fingers tightened round the pencil as a tug of anticipation caught in the pit of her stomach.

Footsteps approached, followed by the soft thud of a briefcase on the parquet wooden floor.

She dragged her head up and flicked her glasses from her forehead to the bridge of her nose, her blue-green eyes adjusting quickly through the glass to recognise the man standing a few feet away from her.

'You looked spellbound.'

It took a moment for his words to sink in. She put the pencil down on the white laminate work top and smiled easily. The vaulted ceiling of the grand Victorian building rose high above their heads like a cathedral. Winter sunshine flooded the hall from the high windows and surrounded his thin frame, catching his silver hair alight as he looked down at her.

'Prof.,' she said, pushing her stool back from the microscope and grinned. 'I'm glad you're here.' She leant to one side and slid a glass flask towards him. It was half full of water and contained several straight hairy stems, thick with yellowish green leaves.

'This specimen came in the overnight post. What do you think?'

The faint sound of traffic drifted in from the streets below. She found the distant noise of the city comforting. It suited her to work high up on the top floor of the King's University tower. Close enough to the city to benefit from the buzz of the best academic minds, but far enough from the streets that she had space to think. In the Herbarium, everything she needed was at her fingertips.

A few hours earlier she'd cut open the battered cardboard box containing the herb. It had arrived via the porter's lodge, addressed to her.

This was unusual in itself. Most specimens were addressed to the professor. As Keeper of the Herbarium, Professor Joseph Bright was known across the country for his expertise in all things green. Gill, however, had only switched from being a postgraduate to an employee just over a year ago. She doubted whether many people knew her name outside the solid university walls.

It was something she needed to work on. A lifelong fascination with plants didn't automatically translate into a successful career as a botanist, however much she wished it could. For that, she needed to prove herself. It was a challenge, juggling her daytime responsibilities as Assistant Keeper – keeping the collections in order and responding to queries – with producing her own work. But she was determined.

Six months ago, she'd had a paper on the role of colour in medicinal plants published by the *British Botanical Journal*. At the time she'd been euphoric, hoping it would be the start of something big. Maybe even a book. But since then her research had been frustratingly slow.

Perhaps this delivery was a promising sign.

She'd taken the box to her makeshift office on the far side of the tower. The Herbarium occupied the entire top floor of the redbrick neo-Gothic building. Two long corridors led off either end of the main hall, linking it to a smaller space on the other side where Gill worked when she didn't want to be disturbed.

The corridors were lined with floor to ceiling cabinets containing the Herbarium's collection of plant specimens. Hundreds and thousands of paper folios, filled with dried and preserved plants from across the world. Gill had already begun working her way through the collections, steadily learning the latin name and uses of every specimen she could lay her hands on.

When Gill opened the box a sweet tang of lemon groves had flooded into her office. Briefly, she closed her eyes. The scent wound around her mind, at once soothing and sharpening her senses. Inside were three bunches of a fragrant herb, tied together with string. Tucked to one side was a sheet of pressed small blue flowers and a note written in scratchy, looping ink.

'A mutation or magic? Paracelsus would be proud.'

There was no signature or return address.

Gill held the note out in front of her and squinted at it through her glasses, wrinkling her nose. What on earth was it meant to mean? She ignored the flash of irritation at the fact that someone would go to all the effort of packaging up a specimen and then write a note to go with it that was next to useless. It didn't contain any sensible information, nothing that would help her to identify the specimen or its uses. Resisting the urge to crumple the note in the palm of her hand and chuck it in the bin, she placed it back in the box.

It was probably from one of the elderly members of the British Herb Society. Gill had a soft spot for the eccentric, and often wildly intelligent, characters who met twice a year to discuss all things herb-related. She remembered lying flat on her stomach next to one of them at the last field meeting, investigating a particularly interesting specimen of the silver moss *Bryum argenteum*, and being quizzed on whether she was doing enough adventurous things with her life. Apparently, she wasn't.

Carefully she unpacked the herb, unbinding it and trimming an inch from the base of the stems before placing them in three separate flasks of water. Taking a fresh blade, she prepared cuttings from five individual stems, pleased when healthy shoots came away cleanly. Then she dabbed the wounds with a white powder and planted them in a row of small black plastic pots. As she pressed the damp soil down, tiny grains of it clung to the whorls of her pale fingertips.

She'd lined up the pots and placed a large plastic dome over them. That was it, there was nothing else to be done but wait. She couldn't resist peering into the dome before she left the room. But there was nothing to be seen. The cuttings remained exactly as she'd planted them, the small shoots each with one or two tender young leaves pointing alert to the roof of the dome. They looked almost amused at her expectation that beneath the soil their cells would begin busily reproducing, hundreds and then thousands of cells dividing to create the complex root system. Like a row of small children playing 'What's the time Mr. Wolf' they feigned complete stillness. And then, when her back was turned, in delight they would begin to move. Slowly, but surely, the roots would stretch down into the soil and slender shoots of life would appear. In a week or so, she would have five new plants.

The professor removed his wire-rimmed glasses with one bony hand then stooped and lifted the flask with the other before closely examining one of the leaves. Curiously he rubbed it, releasing the citrus scent. The crow's feet at the corners of his eyes deepened in appreciation.

'It looks like lemon balm. *Melissa officinalis*,' she said. 'But the colour's wrong.'

He put the flask down. The water around the stems tilted with the movement and caught the sun, refracting and splintering a bright flash of light into the colours of the rainbow. Replacing his glasses, he picked up the sheet of pressed flowers. 'Incredible. What is it? Cobalt, ultramarine?' Lemon balm flowers were usually white or lilac.

She took the sheet from him. The vivid colour popped off the page, tiny blue trumpets waiting to be played by fairy fingers and fairy lips. Her fingers itched to touch the petals, to see if their colour was an illusion. Perhaps when her fingertip made contact with it, the illusion would be shattered and the colour would disappear. She resisted the urge to exclaim out loud in wonder and, instead, put it down.

'I remember seeing flowers this colour when I was a child,' she said.

It was true. The memory struck her without warning, intense and pure. Gill had always thought it was a trick of her mind. That the few times she allowed herself to look back, she'd exaggerated the clarity and colours of those days. The flowers her mother had grown over the deck of the houseboat they lived in. A bright tumble of blue, ranging from pale robin's egg to vibrant azure. But never the exact colour that her mother searched for.

Gill's leg jigged irritably beneath the worktop. She hated looking back. There was no point. She shifted her attention back to the professor, as he spoke.

'It could be down to the mineral content of the soil, strong acid brings out the blue tones. Where did it come from?'

'Postmark looks like somewhere in Herefordshire, or Hertfordshire, it's so water stained I can't be sure.'

'Shame. Why don't you take some cuttings, then you'll get root samples at least?' he suggested.

'Done already. They should grow to a decent size in six weeks,' Gill said.

'Good,' he nodded. 'How's the cellular exam going?'

'Almost there. Doesn't look like a new species. I'll wrap up in a minute, send what I've got to the lab and wait for the roots to grow. But ...' she trailed off.

'Yes?'

'I don't know.' She paused, unwilling to try and put into words something she hadn't yet put her finger on. Then she relaxed. This was the professor, they discussed half thought-out theories, what ifs and but whats, all the time. 'I'm missing something. You're right, the colour can be explained. If it turns out that the cellular structure matches the species', there's no point spending more time on this.' She gestured to the microscope and her pencil sketch. The graphite lines swept intricately and precisely across the page, capturing the impossible beauty and geometry of the cells.

'True.' The Professor's eyes glinted as he waited a beat. 'But what are you going to do?'

Gill glanced up at him, slowly returning his smile. 'It's an interesting herb isn't it? There's no harm in doing a bit more research.' She picked up her pencil, tapping the end gently on the work top. Tap, tap, the sound echoed the rhythm of her mind as she weighed up the options.

She gave a final loud tap, more sharply than she had intended. 'I don't like following a hunch with no scientific basis. It makes me uncomfortable. You've always taught me research is more focussed when instinct is backed up with rational questions, and you're right. I'm struggling today with the rational questions and I don't know why. This specimen's distracting me. Perhaps it's the smell,' she said, as though trying to convince herself that could explain everything.

'Working late again last night?' The professor asked.

She nodded. 'The Nils collection. Flora of Nepal.'

'I wondered when you'd get round to that. Always wanted to do it myself, when I was working for Prof. Marcus. Something more urgent always cropped up,'

'It's not work. Not really,' she said, eyes bright. 'More like a guilty pleasure. There's so many incredible specimens, from a part of the world I've always dreamed of going to.' Her mother used to tell her stories of far-off mountains and exotic flowers to get her to sleep. She'd fancied the idea that a distant ancestor came from Nepal and Gill had been happy to believe it. In the flickering night light she could even see it, sometimes, in her mother's high cheekbones and oriental eyes.

Also, on a more practical note, this collection was one of the few that hadn't yet been reviewed. That meant there was a chance of discovery. A new plant, that could make all the difference to her research.

LEONORA GALE

The Well-Tempered Wife

Synopsis
The Well-Tempered Wife *is a contemporary lit-lite novel, about a pianist who gives up her career after having a miscarriage on stage. She flees London after her husband is found overdosed on a park bench, and revises her high opinion of him twenty years later, when she discovers he is still alive and living with her sister.*

Erica Francis *(beautiful, ethereal) is a virtuoso pianist. Recurrent miscarriages plague Erica and her husband* **Vincent** *(wealthy, debonair), who numbs the disappointment with binges of drink and other women.*

When Erica's sister **Violet** *(sensible, respected trauma-surgeon) and Vincent begin an affair, Vincent confides he has huge debts – banking on inheriting a legacy, claimable on the birth of his first child. Unbeknown to Vincent, Erica is pregnant. Violet brings Erica terrible news that Vincent is dead. The sisters quarrel, irreconcilably. Erica flees London to raise her child in a coastal village.*

At eighteen, Erica's son **Gwilam** *(academic, hiding homosexuality) leaves for London, to study medicine. Attending his graduation, Erica's world is shattered again, meeting Gwilam's friend's parents – her sister Violet, and partner – Vincent.*

Erica agrees to stick to the story that Vincent died, to preserve the tragic-hero father figure for Gwilam. Erica marries **Osian** *(dependable, faithful). On their honeymoon, Osian is killed in a terrorist attack outside Notre-Dame. Erica returns to London to be near Gwilam, who hides a string of gay affairs.*

Vincent's identity is revealed. Erica takes Vincent back. Feeling betrayed, Gwilam moves away. A year later, Notre-Dame burns.

Months later, an accident shatters Erica's wrist. Gwilam visits, and finally tells her he's gay. Both admit to telling sustained lies, and reconcile.

Erica begins composing music suited to her physical constraints, having notable success. In a rare interview, ostensibly talking about music, she beams with pride over her greatest work, her son.

The Well-Tempered Wife

1
London, 1986

The applause filled the auditorium only briefly, before dulling to a muted grumble of 'where's she gone?', and, 'what the devil?' The pianist, after striking the last chord of the *Hammerklavier* had bent forward for a moment on the piano stool, one hand wiping the sweat from her brow, the other clutched tightly to her abdomen. As she stood, she turned to face the audience, as one would expect. But what was puzzling to many in the crowd, was whereas when Erica Francis had walked onto the stage forty-five minutes earlier, they had noted her strikingly upright posture – was that now, at the end, she was crooked. Her previously poker-straight torso was skewed at the hips, and she bent forwards and clutched at herself, as if trying to press in a hernia, or relieve a stitch.

She faced her adoring public, but rather than bestowing upon them a grateful smile of acceptance, bowing, receiving a lavish bouquet of flowers, then reprising the bow with a lower, more emphatic gesture, perhaps blowing a few kisses in dewy-eyed exhilaration – her blank eyes were fixed down on the polished stage floor. Still hunched over, she shuffled sideways away from the piano stool, placed one hand on the glossy black Steinway for a moment's support, and then staggered off stage crabwise, until she was out of view.

She'd pulled a muscle mid-*Hammerklavier* before, which is why the dull ache in her lower-belly barely registered during the performance. Beethoven, with characteristic peppy understatement, had described it as 'a sonata that will give pianists something to do', and the fiendish piece was, depending on whether you took the side of Erica, or her senior professors, either a bravely audacious, or inadvisedly foolhardy choice for her debut headline performance.

The gathered crowd at the South Bank Centre had amongst its numbers a mélange of Erica's contemporaries, who, with their excited chatter and ripped jeans, mildly irritated the serious-minded, regular concert-going members. Erica's father Jacques Legrand, a veteran of the London concert scene, and a respected pianist himself, though never one to have attempted the *Hammerklavier* in public, had returned from his retirement in Honfleur, to see what he was sure would be his daughter's triumph. Her husband Vincent was there, dutifully slicked and suited, though he found her music student friends tiresomely gauche and her professors insufferably stuffy. Unusually though, this evening, he found himself appreciating the undeniable buzz that preceded the performance. His goodwill extended to allowing himself to be clapped on the back by the most tedious of all Erica's fellow musicians, Tarren Joseph, a limpid bore who Vincent suspected had always been itching to get into Erica's pants, only never had the balls to make a move. Letting the pretentious muso-chatter of Tarren and Jacques wash over his head, Vincent was nevertheless intrigued to catch Tarren eyeballing the far corner of the reception foyer, and leaning in to whisper conspiratorially, with the relish of the only one in the know, that he'd spotted Morris Berber from EMI lurking in the shadows. Erica had been certain no-one from a record label would come, and this, Vincent knew, was a monumental nugget that as soon as the performance was over, he would rush to lay at her feet, well before he would let Tarren Joseph get anywhere near her.

It was only on striking the final eight-note B-flat major chord of the fugal fourth movement – that stimuli from the world beyond the hardened resin and blackened ebony keys beneath her fingers, and the looping feedback of inexplicable beauty that her pushing of these wooden teeth produced, came back to Erica. Surfacing, the sensation that rushed in upon her was not one of sound, being neither the woefully underwhelmed polite hand-clap she'd feared, nor the uproarious clamour she'd occasionally dared to imagine. The sensation was in fact wholly disconnected from the audio-visual spectacle of appreciation that the rapt crowd were vigorously delivering, which included the practically unheard of event of Morris Berber standing on his feet and emphatically banging his pale, clammy palms together – but was instead of a rushing warmth and wetness between her thighs, and a tearing ache at some unidentifiable point between her abdomen and pudenda.

The dress of golden silk that she'd so carefully chosen, after fretting whether the spaghetti straps offered enough coverage for her newly heavy breasts, was now stained at the seat with a vermillion Rorschach Ink Blot Test bat-butterfly-moth chimera. This dark stain of ragged miscreation, as if the subject of questionable psychological stability who was assessing the amorphous creature, had taken a kitchen knife and slashed through its hybrid bowels – dripped profusions of brownish-red rivulets from its wing tips, down the length of the back of Erica's gown.

Due to her lateral exit, none in the crowd had spotted this evidence. In the wings, she twisted at the waist and grabbed a handful of her dress, pulling it around to confirm her suspicion. Seeing the stain, a strangulated mew emitted from her throat, and she hurriedly kicked off her high crimson heels, haphazardly gathered the train of ruined silk in her arms, and scurried barefoot back to her dressing room, narrowly avoiding the approach of a concerned and well-meaning stage-hand.

In her dressing room, she pulled the dress over her head, and then peeled down the pair of sensibly beige knickers she had been forced to employ. As she rolled the sturdy fabric down her thighs, fresh blood smeared her skin. She let the soiled granny-pants fall onto the heap of ruined dress, the sodden clump causing the daubed silk to billow out briefly, before settling into a caramel and ruby pyre. She took the white waffle bath-robe that hung on the back of the door, which had, only two hours earlier, been fastidiously employed as a protective layer to shield her glistening dress from any residue resulting from the application of foundation, black mascara and a bright red slick of Chanel's *Premiere Allure* lipstick. Not caring that the white robe would have to be added to the pile of casualties, Erica wrapped it around herself, walked over to the chaise longue, and not bothering to remove the coats and scarf that had been tossed over it, lay down on her side with her legs drawn up to her knees, and waited.

2
London, November 1994

Erica had decided tonight was the night. She wondered if they should go to the annual Dulwich bonfire in Belair Park, where she could whisper the news to Vincent over hot dogs and cups of mulled cider. She'd wait until just before the fireworks began, so amongst the puffa-jacketed throngs of spectators they'd be sure that really, the celebrations were firing just for them. Twelve weeks in, just over, for the first time in – what? Seven or eight years? She had walked to the hospital through Regent's Park that morning, attempting to pace off the nausea through the chilly November air. She was always sick, but this time it seemed unusually severe.

When not pregnant, no matter how many times she told herself she would give anything to suffer the agonies of this woefully misnomered *morning sickness* – that the malady was a joyous privilege she would be happy to go through again – each time, the reality of living it knocked her for six. For weeks on end, her constant companion was an undulating nausea that rose in unbidden waves, hastening a dash to the nearest loo to heave up yellow bile and watery spittle. When not actively hurling, the sickness lay smouldering, a crouching tiger ready to pounce upon any sudden movements. If she should venture to do anything so rash as bend down to pick up a dropped manuscript page, or dare to take the stairs two at a time, she would regret it. On top of the debilitating queasiness, there was the like-clockwork four in the afternoon slump to contend with. Not just the usual office-worker's yawn and stretch, perked up by a cup of tea and a few custard creams – this fatigue would leave her physically unable to hold herself upright. No hot liquid, no mix of refined sugar, palm oil, and simple carbohydrates could even be contemplated. Come the witching hour, she was simply incapable of doing anything other than crawling under the covers to lie still and quiet in the darkened bedroom. It wasn't 'resting', it wasn't cosying down with a good book or listening to an amusing panel show on Radio Four. If she could lie in a state of sensory deprivation for half an hour or so, intensely focused on being absolutely still and absolutely quiet, black-out blinds down, ear-plugs in; the episode would pass. At some point, she would realise with the utmost relief, she didn't feel sick anymore, and would tentatively, without opening her eyes, unfurl herself limb by limb, gingerly opening the tightly curled ball of her body, stretch out on a cool section of bed linen, and fall asleep.

As usual, she had steeled herself for disappointment, for the all too familiar, 'I'm so sorry Mrs Francis,' routine. She had therefore been astounded to find herself lying flat on her back on the sonographer's bed, bladder full to bursting, whilst Dr Hargreaves pushed and rolled the probe head across her abdomen, pressing mercilessly deep onto her barely perceptibly swollen belly. He was silent, his face a mask of concentration, intently studying the screen in front of him, which was tactfully turned away from her field of vision. A few clicks at the keyboard, zoom in, pressing, rolling, pushing on her tender underbelly. She wished it over. She knew what was coming – it was taking too long to be anything other than bad news.

'O.K.' said Dr Hargreaves, breaking the silence. He kept the probe head pressing low on Erica's stomach, in a particularly uncomfortable spot, whilst turning the screen slightly towards her.

'Here's your baby,' he said, pointing at a writhing blob on the screen, 'the little tyke's lying facing into your back at the moment, so giving me a bit of trouble to see everything clearly. But can you see, in the middle, just there?' he gestured to Erica to look, 'that little white flicker, that's the heart beating away nicely.' He paused and smiled down at her, 'everything looks super Erica.'

She had hugged Dr Hargreaves before going – her confidante all these years who'd had, until today, nothing to offer her except confirmation of the worst. She had stopped telling Vincent each time, to avoid the resulting three-day benders, so Dr Hargreaves knew more than her husband how many false starts there had been. Elated, she couldn't bear to descend straight down into the stuffily heated tube station. Instead, she wrapped her scarf around her face against the cold, and strolled out into the crisp breeze of Regent's Park, gratefully gulping in the icy air that seemed to lend each step she took a light bounce, as if she would float up into the bare and leafless mighty oak canopies overhead.

She wandered along the edge of the boating lake, then crossed over the water to the Garden Café, where she bought tea in a paper cup and, contrary to all usual habits, a large and glistening currant bun. She headed outside to the bandstand, and perched, leaning back against the metal balustrade, to watch the idle progress of rented pedalos, through the dangling fronds of the weeping willow monolith that pleasantly framed her view. She sipped the hot, sweet tea, steam rising from the sippy hole in the plastic lid, and delightedly pulled pieces of sticky bun out of the paper bag, devouring them appreciatively. She licked her fingers and thumb between each sugary lump, not minding that her solitary lip-smacking and appreciative slurping drew curious looks from passers-by. Upon screwing up the paper bag, she realised, that for the first time in weeks, whilst upright, at this time in the afternoon, she felt no trace of sickness. Smiling, she sat there, hands clasped around the warm cup, watching frazzled young mothers cajoling and bargaining with their tyrannical little charges, without feeling angry, without trying not to notice them. She smiled at the children, she said 'Hello' to the mothers as they walked by, who without exception politely but cursorily acknowledged her as they took their children's hands to walk purposefully on, for however diminutive and harmless she looked, it still wasn't done to talk to strangers.

As she drained the last drop of tea, she began to feel the chill, so pulling her scarf protectively back up over her mouth, she head off on foot across the park, her step skipping, to catch a taxi home. She would rest, she would nurture, she would prepare. By the force of her will, she would carry this baby to full term and bring it kicking and screaming into the world full of health and life, pink, angry and hungry for her milk. Telling Vincent the news, she would restore his hope, rekindle his love, and mend everything. This unexpected ray of light would bathe everything in its golden glow, draw them together, and mend their heartaches. In the back of the black cab, Erica rested her head back, placed a hand on her belly, and watching the elegant South London streets go by, smiled with delight.

*

The *rat-a-tat-tat* of the front door knocker woke Erica. She started, and realised she had fallen asleep on the sitting-room sofa. She checked her watch, six o'clock, it would be Vincent. She had left a message with Marian at the office for him to be home early if he could, she wanted him sober, relaxed, a dinner at home with the two of them tearily happy together. Odd that he would knock, but not totally unknown for him to forget his house key.

She lightly pattered to the door, stomach fluttering, unable to stop smiling. She undid the heavy latch and swung open the door. Her smile dropped as she saw that upon the step stood not Vincent, but her sister Violet, with a look of such sorrow and foreboding spread across the ashen pallor of her face, that Erica immediately felt the joy and happiness of the day fall down through her torso, her legs, out of the soles of her feet and smash to pieces on the frozen November ground.

'Vi?' still standing in the open doorway, Erica spoke her sister's name trepidatiously.

'E,' said Violet, her voice shaking, faltering, seeming unable to say anything further.

'What is it? Vi?' Erica implored, her trepidation progressing to alarm.

'There's been an accident,' said Violet. It seemed she couldn't get any more words out, but instead, stepped forward and enclosed Erica in a clutching, sobbing, hug. 'I'm sorry E,' she eventually managed to mumble into her sister's neck, 'there was nothing I could do.'

MEL GOUGH

Leap of Faith

Synopsis
South Africa, 1953 – Daniel Blakemore is an Anglican cleric working at a mission. He's been an itinerant priest since World War 2. He's happy with his employ abroad, and being away from home makes it easier to hide his homosexuality.

One day, a new doctor arrives. Eddie Raleigh is young, handsome – and gay in every sense of the word. They bond over the Herculean task of saving the hospital from financial ruin.

But their love dare not speak its name. Daniel is soon reminded that they're playing with fire when the mission hospital's medical director threatens to divulge his secret to his diocese. Fearful and devastated, Daniel ends his budding relationship with Eddie.

When he realises that he's made a terrible mistake, it's too late – Eddie has fallen ill, and has been spirited away.

London, six months later – Daniel returns to his home parish in East London. All trust between him and the medical director had been lost, and for the first time, Daniel is desperate to return home.

Here, his struggles continue. He tries to live the life of an upright parish priest. His widowed housekeeper Betty is just the person to help him build that new life.

Eddie, meanwhile, has restarted his career in the NHS. He works and lives in Northwest London, and is trying to forget the love of his life by having a good time in London's gay underworld.

To Daniel, it soon becomes apparent that he can't be a loving husband to Betty and stepfather to her son. He, too, seeks solace in one of London's secret gay bars, and the arms of strangers.

When Daniel's naivete causes him to take up with the wrong man, fate places Eddie in the right place at the right time. He saves Daniel just in time from being beaten to death, and, after some renewed soul searching the two men emigrate to Australia where they find their happily ever after at last.

Chapter 1

'Father Blakemore?'

The voice calling my name belonged to Nurse Piper who, when I looked up, motioned to me. Matron said, 'I can finish Mrs. Mako's dressing on my own.' I handed her the bandages and she returned her attention to our patient.

When I reached the young nurse she held out an enamel plate, looking harassed. 'Father, I'm ever so sorry. We've overrun at the clinic, would you be so kind and start lunch without me?'

'Of course.' I took the plate from a relieved-looking Nurse Piper. 'If you help Mrs Bhayi first. She's still very weak from her surgery and can't manage alone. You get a head start, and I'll ask Joseph to help me carry up the trays, and then we can do the rest together.'

Mrs Bhayi occupied the bed by the window. The many narrow cots crammed into the ward should have made for a busy, uncomfortable atmosphere. Back home, even before the war, it would've been considered an imposition to share a recovery space with so many. At Providence, nobody thought anything of it, glad to be cared for at all. With colourful shawls and blankets, and a few necessities arranged below the cot, the ward was a cheerful, comfortable place for patients and visitors who conversed in low voices.

Before settling on the low wooden stool by my charge's bed, I pushed the wooden shutter open a crack, tempting in a non-existent breeze. The large, oval rondavel that served as my chapel sat on the opposite corner of the hospital grounds, and not far from it, a run-down, dusty VW bus rusted under a mulberry tree. Not for the first time I made a mental note that the bus had to be seen to. Voices from the yard drifted in on the warm air. Patients and staff were settling down in any available shade with their lunch of fish and mealiepap.

As I settled down on the stool my black shirt stuck to my back, and the dog collar cut into the skin of my neck, unpleasantly soggy with sweat. Adjusting it would just make me look dishevelled, so I focused instead on the tiny, wizened woman dozing on the bed.

I woke her as gently as possible. She wasn't excited about the prospect of food, but after a little coaxing in a mix of Africaans and English, I got her to take a small spoonful of mealiepap. We kept this up for a while, gentle arguments interspersed with little victories when she would open her mouth for another bite.

'Father, a word.'

Mr Hogarth, hospital chief and head surgeon, stood in the doorway, tall and imposing, and motioning at me to step out of the ward. Before I could demur, Sister Genevieve, who had been working nearby, took the plate from me. 'Go on, I'll finish here.' She added, 'But don't be too long, and go right to the chapel when Hogarth is finished with you. It's almost time for service.'

'We got a problem, Father,' Hogarth announced without preamble. His long, narrow face looked drawn, and his small eyes peered tiredly from behind wire-rimmed spectacles.

'Oh?'

'The bastard isn't budging.' Hogarth gave a sigh. 'Finished and klaar. To him, Apartheid is the best thing that's ever happened to his country.'

I ignored the swearing. Not that Hogarth would care either way, but foul language didn't bother me. 'No luck at Broadwick Farm, then?'

My heart sank. The estate belonged to Jasper Fleet, influential landowner and Providence Hospital's biggest problem.

Hogarth gave a snort. 'He wouldn't even see me. His servant barred the gate. I stood out there like a fool.' His face creased in anger. 'That bastard,' he muttered under his breath.

Hogarth reached into his pocket and pulled out an envelope. On the thick, cream-coloured paper I could make out the logo and address of Smith, Alderson & Partners, Port Elizabeth. 'The solicitors' reply,' he explained. They can help prepare a case against Fleet, for the trivial sum of three hundred pounds.' He added with venom, 'Bloody vultures.'

My stomach dropped. 'We can't afford that!'

Hogarth's nostrils flared. 'And preparing the case is just the beginning. Challenging Hogarth's claim that the land Welvyn sold to us for the new hospital site belongs to him will take weeks in court, if not more. ' Hogarth fixed me with his pale, tired gaze. 'That's why I came to you—'

'Sir,' I tried to head him off. 'As you are aware, St Jude's parish, who pay for my stipend here, is one of the poorest parishes in London's East End who is desperately trying to recover from the ravages of war. They beg the money to send a cleric to Providence Hospital from the diocese every year, and will continue to do so. But we don't have access to legal funds.'

'Write to your Archdeacon anyway,' Hogarth said. His eyes were cold like pale diamonds. 'We need the new buildings. We can't go on without electricity, and the well is close to silted up again.' He didn't mention the many thousands of pounds that had already been sunk into the site, where the new foundations sat like so many teeth fallen from the jaw of a huge beast forgotten since antiquity.

I decided to humour him. 'Very well, I'll appeal to Archdeacon Greville's better nature. But,' I added, trying to sound stern. 'Do not hope for a miracle.'

Hogarth sighed. 'I don't believe in miracles. But maybe you can pray for one anyway.' He turned and headed towards his office at the end of the balcony, shoulders slumping with fatigue and disappointment.

I almost felt a twinge of sorrow for the man. I couldn't pretend to like Hogarth much, with his stern personality and stiff demeanour, but his practical, swift and forceful approach was well suited to make the most of the limited resources available. And for the patients, villagers and, yes, myself, I would pray for a miracle. We needed that new hospital site.

At his door, the chief turned back round. 'I nearly forgot a bit of good news,' he said. 'A letter from Cape Town arrived today. The Health Board approved my request for a new doctor. He'll be here any day. A Cambridge man, no less!'

'We will all be grateful for fresh expertise and an extra pair of hands,' I replied.

Some good news at last. We needed the extra help badly, and Hogarth had done well to get it. The administration was stingy with its funds for province hospitals, so this was quite the victory.

I looked at my watch. Worship was due to start in ten minutes. I hurried for the chapel.

Sweat ran down my back when I let myself into the rondavel. Wiping my brow with a pocket handkerchief I opened the ancient, colonial-style wardrobe that held the church paraphernalia. I sent a silent prayer heavenward for a speed lowering of the temperature, feeling guilty about the blasphemy. The last thing I wanted to do was put on another layer of clothing.

The wardrobe door creaked open on wobbly hinges. I slid the white vestment from its hanger, and pulled it over my head. Then I reached for the green stole, which hung from a nail at the back of the wardrobe. I held it for a moment, stroking the frayed golden embroidery. I brought the stole to my lips with a silent blessing and kissed it, before placing it around my neck. Despite being hotter than ever, the ritual of donning the sacred vestments raised my spirits.

As I closed the wardrobe, the chapel door opened and the small, bustling form of Sister Genevieve hurried inside. 'Hello, Father,' she said, giving me a bright smile.

'Sister.' I nodded and returned her smile. Sister Genevieve was my favourite of the half-a-dozen nuns working at the hospital. She was always cheerful, and could brighten a room simply by entering it.

'What did Mr Hogarth want?' Sister asked. She went into the corner where the boxes with hymn books and bibles were stacked.

Deciding on the spot not to upset anyone with more bad news about the land dispute, I said, 'He told me that the new doctor will be arriving any day now.'

Sister Genevieve started distributing the hymn books on the narrow benches. 'Oh, that's wonderful!' she exclaimed. 'We are in dire need of an extra doctor!' Then her face turned serious. 'We were one short today for the early shift. Paula, that student nurse from a dorp by Joburg? She had a letter yesterday. Her older sister was offered a job as a secretary, but it's on the other side of town and she can't get a permit to come into the city every day. She'll have to stay at a house for single black women on the factory premises. So Paula is going home to help her mother, who is elderly.' She sighed. 'Things are getting worse, Father.' I said nothing. There were no words that could explain what was happening in the Union. Sister Genevieve returned to her song books, and I to my preparations.

'What are you opening with today, Sister?' I asked when she opened the piano and flicked through the sheet music that lay on top. Sister had a lovely singing voice and a good ear for music, and her contribution was the highlight of my services.

'I thought we'd start with Abide with Me, for everyone to calm their spirits.' She threw me a quick look. 'It's been a busy week, as you know. And maybe Great is Thy Faithfulness, to wrap things up nicely?'

I nodded. 'Wonderful choices, as always.' She gave me a radiant smile, and I turned towards the desk and tidied away papers, pens and blotter. Then I fetched a large, brilliantly white but slightly threadbare cloth from one of the smaller compartments in the wardrobe. Sister Genevieve came over to help, and together we spread the cloth over the desk that did double duty as altar. The desk, the wardrobe and the old piano had been bequeathed by a local landowner upon his death several years before.

The prayer services did not feature holy communion, so I didn't unlock the smallest compartment of the wardrobe, which held the wafers and wine. Instead, I took two short, stubby candles from a bottom drawer and placed them on either end of the altar. Candles were a precious commodity at the hospital. Jacob always tried his best to procure two matching paraffin candles for me, even when the rest of the hospital had to make do with tallow and the cheap lamp oil that sputtered and smoked.

I lit the candles, saying a quick blessing, to transform the writing desk into a holy place of worship.

People started to arrive. They spoke in low voices. The colourful dresses of the village women who had walked up for worship mixed with the blue and white uniforms of the nurses, and the bright habits of the nuns.

I my back on my congregation to finish my preparations. My bible, a small, well-thumbed leather-bound edition, came from the drawer that held the candles. Before placing it on the altar, I opened the back cover and stroked the yellowed piece of paper that was glued to the cardboard there. Resisting the urge to unfold it, I closed the book and placed it front and centre on the altar.

One last time, I returned to the wardrobe. The small wooden cross I pulled from one of the drawers was my special joy and comfort. It was unadorned, quite discoloured and bore many scrapes and cuts. It had gotten wet many times on the battle fields of France. It had kept me safe then, and had given many dying and wounded soldiers solace in their darkest hour as I spoke their last rites. It had accompanied me to my next calling, bringing comfort to those fighting the many small battles in hospitals like this. It was my physical reminder of the journey that had led me here, and a beacon of hope for an unknown future.

I didn't need to turn around to know that the small chapel was now full. A silence stretched over the room like a comforting blanket, and I could feel dozens of eyes on my back, the anticipation enveloping me. Even the heat was more bearable.

I kissed the cross and put it next to the bible. Then I took a deep breath and straightened up. Everything I was outside this room, all my memories, fears and hopes dropped away.

Listening to the deep silence inside, I stood motionless for a moment. The faint bustle of the hospital grounds still penetrated through the glassless windows, but it could've been another planet. I began my silent prayer.

Oh Lord, though I am unworthy, You are with me. Through my pain and suffering, I turn to You. Your love gives me the strength to go on, now and always.

The prayer was my own creation, not sanctioned by any church. Had another pastor heard it, he would've likely disapproved, maybe even felt troubled. But this was the prayer that lived in my heart. All my services started with its silent recitation, my private moment with God. I had thought it up one night lying before Alsace, and like the cross, the words had been my companions ever since. They were like a tonic, and gave me the strength I needed for the task that followed.

I turned around, arms outstretched. Fifty or so faces looked up at me, expectant, calm. I smiled, then nodded at Sister Genevieve, who turned towards her piano.

'Welcome,' I said. 'Let us pray!'

SEAN GREGORY

Dismember the Past

Synposis
From the bitter rain of Manchester to the heady sun of Malaya, Anthony Burgess seeks inspiration and experience, but what of those left behind and those bound to him for better or worse.

Returning to his home town of Manchester, Anthony is confronted by family he last saw forty years ago when he was a struggling composer, known as John Wilson.

With his wife Lynne, John emigrated to Malaya, in 1954, to teach the sons of wealthy Malayans. They spend their time drinking heavily and falling in love with other people. Both try to leave but find they are bound together. In an attempt to compose a Malayan symphony, John creates characters and scenes that become his first novel.

In 1968, Lynne dies of cirrhosis. Their last time apart was during WWII. With John stationed in Gibraltar, Lynne fell in with the London literati. On leave to confront Lynne about her adulteries, John meets her friend Sonia Brownell (soon to be Orwell) and falls in love.

In 1964, John has another affair. Lynne's health deteriorates and John's career develops in tandem; he sleeps with an Italian translator, Liana. And after Lynne passes, he marries her. Liana and her son, Andrea, move in with John, who becomes Anthony. Haunted by Lynne, he convinces Liana to relocate. They journey through Europe in a Bedford Dormobile, Liana driving and Anthony writing. After months they arrive in Malta. Anthony immediately returns to London to discuss an adaptation of A Clockwork Orange.

Riding high on new-found fame, Anthony finds Stanley Kubrick has terminated their Napoleon collaboration. The script becomes a novel that blends music and literature. His musicality recognised by a conductor; Burgess is commissioned to write a symphony. Travelling America, Burgess composes his greatest work and gathers his distant family for the debut performance.

He flicks the pinched tip of his cigarette onto the Mancunian Way and watches as it is shot down by gobs of rain. The taxi moves beneath new shafts of concrete that punctuate the skyline. Somewhere in all this brutalism is John Wilson's home. They can tear down all they want and build whatever they fancy to replace it, but Manchester can't shift its own smell, its own skin. It's all rouge and blusher on pockmarks.

Overhead, illuminations advertise an asinine, gurning radio disc jockey. Aloft like some great apiarist, his gaudy image punctuates the grey. The drone of inching cars, the drone of the city itself. He dreams of living out his life as an enigma, present only as two words on a dust jacket. *Apis Bombilius.* The dense traffic parts, syphoned off towards Princess Parkway. The taxi circles, Hulme high-rises, Trafford mills, Church of St George, Potato Wharf, and on to Knottmill.

He taps the partition glass, pokes a crisp five-pound note through the grille and stubbornly waits for change. His feet hit the paving with steps punctuated by the crackle of broken glass.

We're just this way. It's a pleasure to have you with us, Mr Burgess. Anita, the assistant manager, walks slightly ahead, setting a pace that she intends to be met.

A pleasure to be here. He stops to take in his surroundings. *This is all very impressive, I must say,* and starts off again to catch up.

They pass the tills and the recommendations; he scans the shelves but can see no works of his own. Above, a sign directs shoppers to the various sections of the shop. Beside an arrow pointing up, *Crime, History, Art.* An arrow pointing straight ahead reads, *Toilets and Fiction.*

Burgess nods towards the sign, *That sounds a fair combination, doesn't it.*

Anita briefly assesses a sign she passes every single day.

Toilets and Fiction, he muses.

In a room off the main floor a couple of tables have been draped in black cloth. Beside the entrance there are two piles of his new book, hardbound.

Can I get you anything? Anita smiles, checking her watch.

Tea. A good cup of English tea.

How do you take it?

Five bags, left to stew well. A drop of milk.

Another polite smile and she is gone. Burgess lights up, using the pot of a wax plant as an ashtray. A tall lad with a look of Larkin straightens out the stacks of books. He rearranges them, fanned across the table. Assessing his work, he tuts, stacking them once more. It is, Burgess thinks, incredible what people will do to occupy the mind.

He sups at the insipid brew; too much milk, not nearly enough tannin. They pride themselves on a good brew up here. In his experience, they do everywhere. The Welsh are particularly proud of their tea-making prowess. Sitting alone, nursing piss-weak tea, he feels undignified and indignant. This is exactly what he had planned to avoid. He made sure to be late but failed to account for the difference between Monte Carlo and Greenwich Mean Time. Too long out of England, too long out of the provinces. And now here he is, alone. Bloody Heinemann and their – he spits tea – marketing strategies.

Hello, Mr Burgess. He can see, just barely, above a stack of hardbacks and paperbacks, the top of a man's face and head. A spire of words held stable by hands at the base and a chin at the apex.

What do we have here?

I was hoping that if I got first in the queue I might persuade you to sign some of my other books, if you could.

With pleasure, with pleasure. Have you waited long?

Not too long, no. The books, Anthony can see from a quick scan, have been arranged in chronological order. *Time for a Tiger* is set before him first, followed by *The Enemy in the Blanket*, *Beds in the East*, and so on.

They tell me, he tells the man, distractedly thumbing to find the title page, *that if you sell these things they're more valuable if it's just the name. My name, that is.*

There's a sudden, almost violent stop. *I would never sell them.*

Who's to say what the future holds. Burgess feels the weight of his own words, faced with the tower of his past. *Shall we keep going?* A copy of *The Worm and the Ring* is placed before him. *Not an easy book to get your hands on. Where did you—*

A place in Alnwick.

Alnwick, indeed. Well. He signs.

I enjoyed MF, the man tells him.

I'm so glad. Nobody else did. Only book I take pride in, as a matter of fact.

The collector seems to bite down on this admission like a fish on a hook. He examines Burgess' face, looking for a tell. *Is that true?*

True? There is scrutiny in that question, in that look. Is this a piece of valuable Burgess information? The book will have to be read again, will have to be put under significant examination, this statement in mind.

Is everything all right? Anita wears a smile only an idiot would take at face value. The queue has been forming and the queue is beginning to get restless.

A collector, Anthony tells her, to clear up any doubt.

If I could ask you to keep it to five items, sir.

Just this one, then. The man takes a hardback from the pile and presents it to Anthony.

He looks it over, *this isn't one of mine.*

Could you. Please?

But this isn't mine. I can't sign someone else's book.

Anita is lifting the remaining books, out of order, four in each hand. Flustered, the collector grabs them from her. Books slip from his grasp, from Anita's arms, falling to the floor. He's on his knees, cursing and scurrying to collect up the books and check their condition.

The tower reformed, the collector raises it and himself up, saying, *Take good care of yourself.*

All the best, Anthony says.

Underneath his own name, he signs dedications to Sarahs, to Brians, he shares best wishes with Ians, Dimitris, Dianes, a Roger. As he gets into the rhythm – flipping two pages in, asking for whom, and signing away – he has to remind himself to look up, that a connection, a real conversation, is what they have all queued for. A youngish woman asks how he finds Manchester now. He gives her the old eye contact, the rehearsed parted-lipped pause, and pushes his hair from his forehead. That's right let them have some of that acerbic wit they've all come for.

Well, of course, my Manchester is the Manchester of internal segregation lines – class, race, religion. But today, the city is a united cause. God bless Mrs Thatcher.

They like that. God bless Mrs Thatcher. You could pay no attention to the papers, stay out of the country for years, and still rely on the collective resentment of the powers that be.

This, for instance, raising his hands up, *was Kendals in my day. A bazaar of household goods, soft furnishing, and electrical appliances. I was brought here on day trips, as a child, just as others were taken to the zoo. We'd wander the aisles, my stepsisters and me, staring at all those foreign objects. Now, of course, this is a home for books, which I think is a very worthy enterprise for a building. I like to think of bookstores and libraries as my second homes. A part of me always remains (as long as I'm still in print).* Very good, let them believe there is always a bit of him here in the North, even if the man himself is drinking Aperol cocktails on the Monte Carlo seafront. Book signed, the woman gratefully thanks him and moves on. Anita puts down a fresh mug of tea, thick and the colour of the Bridgewater Canal.

How's your hand going?

Oh, my hand's all right, but I'm forgetting how to sign my name. I start writing the title and then it sort of slips.

Any Old Burgess, she says.

Yes, something like that.

You're our Jackie. An accusation. A disbelieving statement. Somewhere in there is a question. Anthony looks up at an ancient man, a practically dead man, who peers back through sunken eyes. He knows this look well, the bloody Mancunian glare. Think you know something, pretentious bastard, it said. The words *bookstores and libraries are my second homes* repeat, growing increasingly louder in his mind. The undead is flanked by two others. All three dressed in shades of brown-beige. Polyester coats, pockets torn, stained at the cuffs and neck. Man-made, then, not figments.

He holds his nerve. *I'm sorry?*

Our Jack. I'm your cousin, Bert. Albert Dwyer. This is our Agnes' usbint. The relic beside nods his pale leather skull. A foolish gawper, more disturbed by the amount of learning that besieges him than this impromptu family reunion. Anthony nods politely and turns to the third of this timeworn triptych. A woman, rippling with layers of skin, beady eyes peering out. The fat softens her wrinkles somewhat, though does nothing to hide her years.

And who, smiling at her now, *is this?*

Wull, our Agnes, in't it. Of course, it is. *Do thee not 'member us, Jackie?* That fucking name. He had crossed continents to escape the smear of *Our fucking Jack.*

I'm sorry. It's, well, I wasn't expecting you. Should I have been expecting you? What did they want? Money, he supposed. But for what, why, was money owed? They could not expose anything he had not already revealed himself. Maybe they thought it only right that the pretentious bastard should put his hand in his well-tailored pocket and draw out a few crisp notes for them what got left behind. That'd be right. Drag them down what thinks theys better than the rest.

Agnes saw it in't paper. You bein' here, like.

Well, I must say, he says, words failing him.

Our Jack! Our Bert whistles. Not impressed, more of a case of what the hell happened.

Elsie died, Agnes pipes up. John saw the comic scene immediately. This geriatric woman (his very own stepsister!), reeling off every name of everybody she could think of what had died since the last time she'd seen their Jack.

Dismember the Past

Well, John says, *it was. What a surprise to see you all. Bert, Agnes, ehm?* The relic nods receptively to Ehm.

Shall we wait? Bert says.

Wait?

For you finishing? Tom's Chop 'Ouse is just rount corner.

Ay, John says.

We'll get you a pint in, Jack. For old times and that.

Relic Ehm lights a roll up and John watches as they expire in a cloud of smoke, towards the Natural History department.

Apparitions spent, an unsigned book is placed in front of him. *And who are you then*, he asks, *me daughter? Some long-lost niece?*

What had they, he signs and hands the book over, come here for? Forty years must have passed, flicking to find the right page, since the last time he'd seen any of them. He had assumed, *Thank you for coming*, that they'd all be dead by now. But here they had stood. The murmur in the room, the sound of the city outside starts to converge to a dull tone, at *440 hertz*. He grasps a book by the spine, *Who should I make it out to*? He signs, John Wilson. He stares at the page. Any old Wilson. The words are an aberration. John takes his pen and draws a picture beside the name – sunken cheeks, double chin, bags under the eyes, hair manic, swiped to the right.

I'll get a fresh one, Anita says in her cheery, not cheery manner.

John pinches the top corner of the page and pulls, tearing the first stitch. He tears again and again – scythe, scythe, scythe. John fucking Wilson.

Outside, Manchester rain runs as only Manchester rain can. Some of the staff have been coerced into giving him a nice little send off. One of them asks for a copy of *A Clockwork Orange* to be signed.

Anita hands him a branded Waterstones' umbrella. *You're sure I can't get you a taxi?*

No. No taxis. He waves her off and waves them farewell, walking down Police Street. The staff watch, some mystified, others suppressing laughter, as the old man of letters, one of Manchester's prodigal sons, struggles against wind and rain to lift his umbrella, dragging a suitcase behind him, off into the city.

Cut up with broken glass, the bottom of his suitcase ricochets off askew paving. Everything seemed too new – shops he doesn't recognise, restaurants recently opened – yet if he lifts his head above street level, the tops of the buildings are old and familiar. He reaches Cross Street. Down there is the Cathedral, the River Irwell, and Hanging Ditch, where he once had a job playing piano. Before the war, all before the war. To the South East, his childhood home, his school, the university he attended. Brunswick Inn, where his first symphony was obliterated in the blitz.

To his left, the Chop House and people he shares nothing with except bleached out memories. There is money owed, he remembers that now. £100 from Agnus Toilett, borrowed some forty years prior. Do they intend to get it from him today? What is the interest on a debt like that? The lights turn red, he crosses Cross Street. The rain isn't helping. He has to shift himself, the case clacking behind, to dodge puddles forming. He is lost and not lost. The rain that had been was merely prelude to that about to fall.

John clacks his suitcase into the City Arms. It looks familiar. But then pubs arouse familiarity. He orders a pint and sees himself as a lad, sat at a table drawing pictures of barmaids, while his dad talked up his piano playing skills. The beer is sharper than John had hoped for. The sides of his mouth seem to swell with every gobful. It is not good beer. Joe Wilson would start all confident like, pulling out sheet music he could hardly read to give a taste of his repertoire. He'd try to time it so he was having a tinkle on the high keys just as the landlord came through. Lovely joanna, he'd tell them.

Do you still have the old joanna? John asks the barman.

Not 'ere, mate. You must be thinking of next door.

I was sure my father played here; piano against that far wall.

Could of, he replies. *But A've never heard of nobody playin' piana in here. You play?*

In my own way. I'm more a composer.

Oh aye, he says.

The landlord, I take it?

Dad is.

My dad too, Anthony says. *The Golden Eagle up in Miles Platting.*

The barman takes a pack of peanuts from the rack, revealing the naked midriff of a girl, her head poking out above two packs of dry roasted. *Never heard or'it.*

Not anymore, of course, Anthony says. *That's long over.* He wants to say more and hear more of Manchester, but the man, no more than thirty he guesses, looks disinterested. Time to sup up and move on. *Give me some of those nuts too*, he says. *Originally from Oldham, are you?*

You what?

Oldham. I can hear it in your voice. Flattened diphthongs.

The barman eyes him. *When I were little. Been here a few years now.* Anthony knows the look: who the fuck is this posh prick?

It struck Anthony that the man was in fact a boy, Manchester being a hard city to grow up in. He now put him at around fifteen, sixteen, pulled out of school to learn the family trade. *I must get going*, he says, though he doesn't move except to hand his empty glass over the bar. *How do you like growing up in a pub?*

It's alright, I suppose.

I remember the sound of several pianos all crashing along at the same time, three different pieces being played. He thought he'd written all this out of himself. *The regulars used to give me a penny, a shilling if I snuck down late enough. Here you got, Little Jackie. I used to run down the stairs first thing in the morning and piss in the men's trough.* A fresh pint placed in front of him, he tastes, much better.

We 'ad a jukebox for a while, the lad says, *but the regulars just complained about kids putting the same song on over and over again.*

The pub wasn't my father's, it was my step-mother's pub, which she inherited from her dead first husband. My father just worked there. You need a male presence, don't you.

The lad lifts the bar flap and goes off to collect empty glasses sat upon empty tables.

My mother had died, John continues. *She died when I was very young.* He raises his glass to the Manchester dead. *She was very young too, though I didn't think that for a long time. The old die, don't they. It's not the role of the young to pass away.* No, he thinks, watching the lad feed coins into the fruit machine, youth has no interest in death. *I perceived in myself, when my wife died, a great loneliness. A loneliness left by her death. And, I thought, what loneliness have I carried all my life, brought about with the death of my mother. I was just a babe, just a small thing. I remember her, you know. I remember her lying there, my sister too. The hand of death can never be forgotten, even when you are so very young.*

John looks over the many spirits in their many optics, waiting to be poured, one measure at a time.

AISHA HASSAN

The Other Son

Synopsis
Set in modern day Lahore The Other Son *is a story about Lalloo, a young man who wants to rescue his parents from their life of servitude – but the brick kiln owner owns his parents, and wants him too. Exploring indentured labour in brick kilns, it is the story of the human will to survive no matter the odds, and the ability of every person to carve out their own destiny.*

The kiln owner murdered Lalloo's brother for speaking out against the family's exploitation and Lalloo was sent away as a child for fear the same fate would befall him. When his parents need money for his sister's dowry, Lalloo resolves to get it for them. He fails to get a loan from his employer, Omer, then tries to blackmail and eventually rob him. Affronted by this audacity from a mere servant, Omer hires the local mafia to have Lalloo killed.

Lalloo is shot while he is driving and his car falls into a ditch. Omer's daughter Yasmin is also in the car and a bullet hits her, leaving her paralysed. Omer is crippled with guilt, as he ordered the shooting that maimed his beloved daughter. Lalloo sells his kidney, fakes his death and smuggles his parents out of the kiln to a new life in Karachi where they live in hiding. Omer is the kiln owner and responsible for Lalloo's brother's murder. By escaping him Lalloo manages to finds closure on his brother's death but he has had to leave behind his friends, the woman he loves, and his beloved city of Lahore.

The Other Son

Chapter One
When Lalloo was six years old he fell into an open sewer. He'd been following Jugnu as usual. This was a lifetime ago, before they'd moved to the bhatti. The brothers ran through the maize fields surrounding their village, trying to keep warm on a winter's day. The maize was ready to be harvested. It grew over Lalloo's head, the stalks so tall he couldn't see Jugnu up ahead, could only hear him as they both trampled through the field before the farmer caught them. Ami's warning to keep his clothes clean was pounding in his ears. His rubber flip flops slapped against his

The Other Son

heels and his lungs hurt as he tried to catch up with Jugnu's voice laughing and teasing, pulling him forward.

He heard Jugnu come to a sudden stop. Lalloo smelt it before he saw it. The sewer was three feet wide and full of black, barely flowing sludge. The cloying smell flared his nostrils and clung to him. Jugnu only hesitated a few seconds before he was off, flying up and over, shouting his encouragement behind him. Lalloo faltered, seeing in the frothing blackness what was at stake. There were floating objects in it. One seemed like the bloated carcass of an unfortunate animal. But Jugnu was already on the other side ready to run off again.

Lalloo retraced his steps so he could take a huge run up. He held his breath against the all-enveloping stench and ran. He jumped and flailed. Then his feet splashed and he was sinking, immersed in the black stench. He pushed himself up and found air. He spluttered. The foul blackness was in his mouth and throat and he retched. He stood on tiptoe to keep his head from going under. Jugnu's shouts made him squeeze his eyes open enough to see a hand reaching down to grab him. He stumbled over and clutched it and Jugnu half pulled, half dragged him onto the bank. On all fours on dry ground he retched again. He tried to wipe his face with his hands but it was everywhere, on his hair, inside his nose and ears, every inch of his body was covered in sticky sludge.

They had no choice then but to walk home. They made an odd couple, Jugnu, tall and lanky, and the small black furry monster that was Lalloo leaving a trail of oozing blackness behind him. He had expected Jugnu's mocking laughter, or at the very least some gentle teasing, but Jugnu knew better. Lalloo's teeth ached from keeping his jaw clamped shut, partially to stop his chin trembling and because he dared not open his mouth, in case more of the foul blackness made its way inside.

Shabnam took one look at them and shrieked, a sound halfway between a scream and a laugh. She ran off shouting. 'Ami, look what Jugnu brought home!'

Their mother came to the door, dishcloth over one shoulder, a wooden spoon in her hand, thunder in her voice. 'Is this what you do when I ask you to keep your clothes clean?'

She marched Lalloo to the bathroom and made him strip. He stood while she poured bucket after bucket of hot Dettol water over him until eventually the glutinous black started washing off. Then she scrubbed him with a brush and more Dettol water.

With the Dettol came the scolding. 'How many times have I told you to stay away from those sewers, could you not find any other place to play? They're filled with raw sewage, and chemical waste from the fields, and animal dung, and Khuda knows –'

'Ami –' Jugnu tried to interrupt her but to no avail.

'All the illnesses in the world in one place and you choose to jump right in! And don't even get me started on the rats and –'

'Alright Ami, you'll make him ill just thinking about it.' Jugnu did then what he always did, deflected their mother's anger away from Lalloo on to himself.

She rounded on him. 'And you! You're supposed to look after your younger brother, not lead him jumping over sewers. He's only six! He could have broken his leg. And what will I do if he gets sick?'

'You should have seen it Ami, our Lalloo went in, and a kaala bhoot came out. I couldn't even recognise him. You know like Superman getting changed, this is Lalloo's disguise.'

Ami tutted at him and shooed him out of her way, but she managed a smile. Jugnu didn't miss a beat. He turned to Lalloo. 'You're a superhero little brother, we'll call you kaala bhoot man. But we're gonna have to do something about this disguise, it really stinks!'

So that even Lalloo, whose eyes prickled with the humiliation of his fall and the pain of his skin being scrubbed until it was raw and who knew he'd never be able to get the smell out of his hair or the taste out of his mouth, even Lalloo was laughing by the end of it. From then on, Jugnu called him his kaala bhoot – his little black monster.

Lalloo pressed his forehead against the mini bus window. Today was the day all the memories crowded in. That had been fifteen years ago. He'd screwed up his eyes to keep the memories at bay, but this one refused to go away. He was on his way to the bhatti. He would have given anything not to go, today, on the worst day of the year. But they were expecting him. It was a family tradition of theirs. Every year, this little trip. Some families had elaborate Eid celebrations or basant parties. Their family had today. The mini bus braked and threw him forward off his seat. He grabbed the metal bar across the window to steady himself. Lahore was shrouded in a thick smog which it couldn't shrug off. Lalloo could taste the dank staleness as it hung in the air. Even the sun was covered in a grey dupatta, leaving her silhouette visible but her heat veiled, casting a morbid light on the day.

He got off at his stop and wrapped his jacket close around him to ward off the chill. The smog was making a determined effort to crawl into his clothes and lay its chilly essence into his bones. The road turned into a dirt path with fields on either side. The soil here was red and loamy, excellent

The Other Son

for making bricks. With each step he took, the fine dust settled on him – first his chappal, then his shalwar, making its way up his body. He breathed it in too, the familiar smell hitting home. By the time he came to Chakianwallah, his white shalwar kameez was steeped in red.

The bhatti chimney loomed up dark and ominous. He sensed the evil eye of the chimney on him, watching him – the one who got away. 'You will come back,' it whispered. Despite the smog Lalloo felt its menacing heat. He bowed his head as he passed, refusing to look at it.

His parents' hut was in the shadow of the chimney. Dusk had not yet descended, but their windowless hut was as dark as ever. As he entered he could hear a dull thudding. It took a few moments for his eyes to adjust and he saw his mother crouched down on her haunches, rocking back and forth. Every time she rocked, she hit her head on the mud wall of the hut, sometimes gently, at other times with considerable force.

'Ami?' he hurried to her and pulled her away from the wall, cradling her body in his arms as if she were a newborn bird, helpless and precious and liable to break. Even muffled in his arms, she continued to rock. He longed to tell her he'd take care of her, stitch up the torn fabric of her life and get her out of there, but she wasn't in a state to listen and he knew he couldn't keep his promise. Jugnu hadn't been able to do it, and nor could he. So he just held her. He looked around and saw Shabnam sitting in the shadows.

He called her but she didn't answer. He called again and she looked up surprised, as if she'd been so lost in her thoughts she hadn't seen him enter. She came up to him.

'I tried to stop her, she's been like this for hours.' She touched Ami's hand, her voice creased with worry.

'Bati jalao, it's getting dark,' said Lalloo.

His sister lit the gas lamp, casting more shadows than light into the recesses of the hut. Pinky came and joined them. She was just a child, but even she knew the burden of this night. Lalloo searched through the darkness.

'Where's Abu?' They had finished work for the day. Abu should have been there.

Shabnam shrugged and Pinky shook her head.

'Here, come and sit with Ami.' There was an urgency in his voice as he transferred his mother into Shabnam's arms and got up to search outside.

He found his father behind the hut. Abu held a shovel in one hand and was crouching over a small object on the ground. As Lalloo approached, the loud speaker in a distant mosque crackled to life, and the muezzin started the Azaan.

Allah u Akbar, Allah u Akbar...
Abu stood up as if answering the call to prayer.
...Allah u Akbar, Allah u Akbar...
But instead of raising his hands to his ears, Abu raised the shovel over his head.

The muezzin continued to bear witness there was no god but Allah, and Abu brought the shovel down with all his might on the packed earth, as if he were still working, preparing the clay to make bricks. Lalloo hurried over to see Abu lifting the shovel from the red earth to reveal the crushed body of a sparrow, its spindly legs crooked underneath it. Abu raised the shovel above his head again as the muezzin urged the faithful on.

'Abu!' Lalloo called out, staying his father's hand. Abu sagged and let Lalloo take the shovel from him. He didn't acknowledge Lalloo's presence. Despite the cold, sweat peppered his forehead and ran down the sides of his face. He was wearing a thin cotton shalwar kameez and his back was sodden.

His voice shook as he spoke. 'I brought us here, I may as well have killed him with my bare hands.'

...La illaha ill Allah. The muezzin finished, plunging them into silence.

Lalloo led Abu to the charpai outside the hut and fetched him a glass of water, finding his own hands were shaking.

When Shabnam came out, Lalloo pulled her aside.

'Is he ok?' she asked, nodding towards Abu.

Lalloo shook his head. He hesitated. 'Do you think we should maybe not go this year?' He kept his voice low and tried to keep the shock out of it.

'Not go?' she stared at Lalloo.

'Look at them, I'm not sure they can take it.'

She looked towards the hut and when at last she spoke her voice was weary, too old to belong to his younger sister. 'They take it every day in this awful place.'

Lalloo had been dreading this day and yet every year his parents' reaction seemed to get worse. 'Yes, but –'

'They need this Lalloo. Today of all days.'

As if overhearing their conversation, Abu stood up and looked at them. His expression was lucid, his intent clear.

'Let's go!' he commanded.

Shabnam and Lalloo exchanged a glance before she led Pinky and Ami out of the hut. With a nod, they set off. Lalloo took off his jacket and tried to wrap it around Abu, but Abu refused. Lalloo snuck a glance at Abu as they walked. Abu had always been thin and wiry and as strong as a bullock. Now he was shrunk with grief and age. When Lalloo was a boy, Abu had loved feeding the sparrows. A piece of naan, a half mouthful of roti, even a spoonful of rice; whatever he could spare, Abu would leave out for them.

The neighbouring huts were already plunged into darkness. Used to the mild winters and oppressive summer heat of the Punjab, the villagers were ill equipped to deal with the smog that clung to every surface and sucked away the warmth. They hunkered down, exhausted from the day's labour, as if barricading themselves indoors would offer them protection.

Lalloo and his family walked past the huts, past the never-ending rows of red bricks piled four bricks high, laid out to dry. They left the bhatti behind and kept walking. An hour later they arrived at the edge of a large cemetery. They were covered in a sprinkling of red dust, as though welcomed with showers of rose petals.

Lalloo led them single file past the great banyan tree growing out of the middle of a grave, the ditch filled with stagnant water and rubbish, and the multitudes of tombstones, until they came to a grave marked only by a solitary stick of wood. The stick was tilted, almost fallen to the ground. Lalloo reached out to straighten it, trying to keep his hand from trembling.

They raised their hands in silent prayer. Shabnam took out red rose petals from the plastic bag she carried and let them fall on to the grave. Seeing the drops of red on the parched ground, Ami cried out and sank to her knees, as if willing the earth to take her. Lalloo was glad he couldn't see her face in the dark.

A breeze picked up the sickly pungent whiff of the petals and rushed it at Lalloo making him want to retch. He didn't think it did them much good to linger at the cemetery. The memory of that night was beaten into their minds with fear, fire and cricket bats. He reached down to take Ami's hand. 'Challo Ma, time to go.' Her hand was cold, her skin rough and cracked. She didn't move. He placed an arm across her shoulders. Her body was so thin, she felt brittle. He pulled her to her feet to lead her away. Shabnam and Pinky followed behind with Abu. The children led their parents back to the bhatti. Back to their hut like prisoners to their cell, held captive by their memories. They would be at work again tomorrow, up before dawn come hail, fog or burning sunshine.

They unrolled the bedding on the packed mud floor of the hut and lay down to sleep. Lalloo lay there, parents either side of him, forcing himself to stay awake. It was the same every year. In this upside down world, fathers murdered sparrows and children led their parents; one son couldn't bear to return home and the other was buried in the middle of the night.

The anniversary of Jugnu's death was the only night Lalloo would sleep in his parents' hut. They didn't have a choice. They lay in the same hut, yards away from where his brother's warm broken body had been left fourteen years ago.

CHRISTOPHER HOLT

The Good Steward

Synopsis
Twenty years after discovering the 'Genesis Particle', Molyneux has changed the world. All physical matter can now be synthetized from energy alone. Agriculture, forestry and mining are unnecessary. Animals are not needed for food and clothing. Factories no longer seek raw materials from natural sources. Gabriel Molyneux, 'the Good Steward', uses his vast royalties to purchase all the abandoned farms and mines for the rewilding of animals in his 'Innocence Zones'.

* * *

Mark Harris, a former army major, now a vicar, agonises over the hordes of creepy 'Stand Starers' who gate-crash his wedding services. To the StandStarers, every public event is a 'Happening'. This also applies to people who are 'different'. Celebrities, buskers, entertainers and artists are never seen in public. Fear rules.

The Archbishop of Canterbury commissions Harris to negotiate with Molyneux who wishes to buy up ruined abbeys to extend his rewilding projects. They meet up at his Complex at Dungeness where Molyneux expresses his disappointment that although human beings now possess all the raw materials they need, they continue their cruelty towards animals and mindless destruction of the planet. Harris suspects that the Good Steward has become a dangerous fanatic.

When David Ewart, a former employee at the Complex, pleads with Harris and his family, to avoid all products containing Molynite, they realise their lives are at risk.

They secretly board an old Thames lugger and take to the English Channel. Next day they discover there are no other ships in sight or evidence of human activity on shore. They realise with horror that Molyneux has reversed his synthesis programme and human life is all but extinct.

Without Molynite in their bodies the Harris family have survived. Their hope is to make contact with other people who might still be living in remote regions elsewhere on the planet.

Greenland

She raises her long neck to sniff the wind. The scent is stronger now. They're close. Too close. Gaunt starving males, ravenous for her cub.

Her one hope is the open sea.

The beach is littered with silver-white driftwood and plastic waste but there's not the barest glint of life, not even a seagull. It's as desolate as the planet Mars. Rags of snow freckle the low cliffs where the melting permafrost trickles down to stagnant pools.

The she-bear finds it hard-going. The icy pebbles are slipping, creaking and crunching under her six hundred pounds weight. The cub is faring worse. With soft juvenile fur on its soles, it skids and slides after its mother, following her blindly into the sea where plastic bottles, lift and fall in the turbid foam.

By dog-paddling and using their rear legs as rudders, the bears swim out to where the mother's instinct tells her they should find the large floes.

But three hours and twelve sea miles later, there is no ice, just rolling billows and blinding spindrift. She slows to allow the cub to paddle up close so they can swim on side by side.

A further six miles and they confront a stifling foetid mass forcing them to dive to three fathoms. Each time they resurface, the filth clings to their fur and they have to dive again.

Just when they are nearly dead from the toxic sulphuretted gas, their lungs swell with a blast of pure air as they are lifted high among the towering crests of the polar current which sweeps them eastwards.

One

Harris scribbles away, shielding his hand from prying eyes. Handwriting is becoming eccentric. He risks becoming a Happening.

Woman – in her fifties – lean as greyhound – tight navy blue tracksuit – sways down aisle – eyes fixed on step – counter worn around wrist like a single handcuff – keeps mouth open – creepily white teeth –

He scowls as he detects an acid tang in the carriage. The two garrulous old men in front of him are devouring vinegar flavoured crisps.

– thank God it's not hot food – just the whiff of it on public transport sets me gagging –

'You're too precious,' says the Prosecutor. 'And for an ex-soldier too! You should be ashamed.'

'I don't like these people,' thinks Harris.

'As a priest, you're not meant to like them. You're meant to love them,' says the Prosecutor.

Harris goes on scribbling.

– 2 girls – both got on at Exeter Central – one putting on her make-up – other slumped against window half asleep – mouth open – slack– slack – slack!

'You're becoming a grumpy old man. You've been out of the army nearly five years and you still can't cope with civilians,' says the Prosecutor.

Harris looks around him. Most of the passengers are caught up in mesmeric fascination with their smartphones. Others are typing on lap tops.

– fingers slipping over the keys like pond skaters – chilled souls – never speaking – no-one speaking to anyone.

'But are you so different?' asks the Prosecutor.

At Feniton a puggish-looking man in an ill-fitting brown suit boards the train and hovers around the luggage hold. Despite the seats available, he remains standing. His stance is hostile and his eyes stay fixed on his tatty red suit-case.

like a possessive guard dog – writes Harris.

The crisp eaters have torn open another bag, this time it's cheese and onion. Harris wants to shout*: '*Some people are as piggish as they look!'

'But then everyone would see your dog collar and mutter something like – No wonder the churches are empty!' says the Prosecutor.

'Not St Aethelthryth's.'

'That's rather prideful of you,' says the Prosecutor.

'It's true though, you can't deny it.'

The step – counting woman returns from the front of the train. She glowers at Harris as she passes.

– frustrated cheetah pacing in long cage –

Now he spots something else.

– look at THAT! – some buzzard of a flying insect above the crisp eaters – ... don't believe this – another – and two more – and they still don't see them – dear God, on the ceiling above their heads – a dozen more of them – huge buggers – and no one even notices –

His eyes switch to one passenger who's looking steadily in his direction. Without looking down at his notebook, Harris writes blindly:

– dumpling of a man – greasy yellow T shirt, skinny black shorts, baseball cap back to front – eyes on me – ever since Honiton – thought he was just bored – (everyone stares at vicars) – still won't take his eyes off me – worse, worse and worse – I'll swear he's a Stand-Starer.

He crosses out *Stand-Starer* and writes *Busybody*. He's got to be accurate. The man's not a Stand Starer. Yet.

It was Charlotte who had given him the note-book. 'So you can be more mindful, dad,' she'd said.

'Mindful?'

'Well my version of mindfulness anyway. Mindfulness is all the rage. Jotting things down will get you into the habit of seeing, *really honestly* seeing and experiencing the world about you – especially the little things. It forces you to live in the present. It might even help you spice up your sermons.'

'OK.'

'So you *will* write in it? Just flash impressions, no need for punctuation or even much thought, only what you see and experience, nothing else.'

'Yes, I will.' He'd smiled.

'Promise?'

'Promise.'

Every day?'

'Every day.'

That promise was made three months ago and Harris finds it surprisingly easy to keep.

– every man should be blessed with a sixteen-year-old daughter like Charlotte –

Two

Two young men both with beards pass Harris as they lumber further down the train carrying blue crested back-packs. He supposes they must be university students. 'Unbelievable,' he heard one say to the other. Did you see that? In this age of unbelief – a genuine vicar still wearing a black shirt with a dog collar.'

'And troubled by your own unbelief,' says the Prosecutor.

'No, I'm a believer but like the father of the sick boy in Mark's Gospel, I need help with my unbelief.'

'A great deal of help I should say. And let's be honest, despite your dog collar, you don't even think like a vicar, you certainly don't look like one, You're too hard-bitten, too world weary Just see your reflection.'

It's true. Reflecting in the train window is not the convivial image of a country clergyman, but the tight square jaw, tense cheek muscles, deep lines and piercing eyes of a professional soldier.

The cruel sun of the Middle East has eroded his skin making him look older than his forty-eight years but he has never abandoned his military grooming. His hair is cut square at the back and sides with a parting as straight as a Roman road.

'And let's be honest,' says the Prosecutor. 'They may *call* you the Reverend Mark Harris but you're neither revered nor reverent. I suppose that's what today's meeting in London is all about. They're out to sack you, Harris. Not before time, I'd say.'

Harris opens his wallet and takes out the Lambeth card once more. The crest is beautiful in its elegant simplicity, just an archiepiscopal staff embossed with four gold crosses on an azure shield.

'The Reverend Mark Harris is invited ...'

Invited?

Untrue, damnably untrue. It's not an invitation. It's a command. He's been ordered! That's the proper word for it, *ordered* – ordered to attend an 'Extraordinary Assembly'. Why the hell don't they say what they mean, for Christ's sake?

'Your blasphemy proves my point,' says the Prosecutor. 'You're not cut out to be a priest.'

He wonders if his wife would agree. Perhaps she'd wouldn't be all that disappointed if they sacked him. When he left this morning Connie had wished him 'good luck' but he knew from the tone of her voice that she thought church matters don't count for much in what she always called 'the real world'.

'That's what comes from marrying an atheist,' says the Prosecutor.

Connie's not an atheist. She's a seeker.

'Well, if you want my opinion.'

I don't.

This morning the family had been in a rush. When he was racing down the stairs Connie was already reversing the car to take him to the station. Luke had called out to him, as he pulled on his school blazer. 'Have a cool day in London, Dad.'

'Carpe Diem,' mumbled Charlotte without looking up from her phone.

'Go for it, Dad,' said Luke. He even had the nerve to pat him on the shoulder. 'You need a bit of time out, anyway.'

'Time out?' His children think he's off on a jolly.

Three

Connie had met her husband in a camp by the Euphrates when Mark Harris was an army lieutenant and she was a young doctor volunteering with Medicins sans Frontieres. Three months later they were married.

That was nineteen years ago and now Mark's left the army and she's become a vicar's wife. Like everything she does, she's risen to the role but she knows that her involvement in the church is hypocritical and the deception is draining.

Yet she adores living at the vicarage. It's late seventeenth-century, and the upkeep is a challenge. Small things, like repairs to curtains or basic plumbing she can do herself. Her hands are quick and instinctive and, despite her husband being an ex-Royal Engineer, she finds it less fuss to do the practical things herself.

But with the increasing hordes of Stand Starers, Connie, like everyone who has practical skills, keeps them a family secret. It wouldn't do to let it be common knowledge that she was an accomplished wood carver. One whisper on social media and the Stand Starers would be down on the vicarage by the hundreds squirming to get inside her shed – not to observe but just to, well, 'stand and stare' in zombie-like quiescence.

It's not just the Stand-Starers, she thinks, inactivity is becoming the norm. Millions of people who would get so much more out of life if only they summoned up the energy. But they don't, they really don't. With so many on the Universal Wage they don't need paid work so they become perpetual tourists, always booking up yet more coach trips and ocean cruises until finally they give up doing anything to amuse themselves at all.

The laziness is pervasive. Connie is often feeling more tired than usual. Mark is tired too, though he won't admit it, nor will Charlotte and Luke who are sometimes in bed by eight-thirty.

Four

Connie owns the surgery in Exeter and always arrives an hour earlier than everybody else. She's even earlier this morning, because she's had to drop Mark off at St David's Station.

As it's Monday, she first checks that the consulting rooms have been cleaned properly over the weekend. 'Cleansed' is the word the company uses. The stainless steel instruments gleam under the blue fluorescent lights, the computer screens glisten and every keyboard has been softly brushed free of dust and human hairs.

Next she goes out to inspect the waiting room, where the green ergonomically correct chairs are set precisely six inches apart. By the far wall there's an impressive tropical aquarium. Neon fishes and rosy tetras glide among the drifting strands of Java ferns and weave quickly between the two silver columns of ascending bubbles.

But today as she approaches the tank, she is mystified when all the fish cease their circumvolutions and come right up close to the glass. Surely, they can't see her. They must be staring at their own reflections.

Something about their behaviour makes her uneasy. Instinctively she steps back. The fish swim off to form a single shoal and return to the glass.

The Good Steward

As Connie moves away, she has the ridiculous feeling that they have won a kind of victory.

Now she checks the new magazines flicking through them for any defaced or torn-out pages. In the latest edition of *Coastal Pics,* there is a double-spread advert where a youthful mandroid with an athlete's body and blazing smile is holding out a beach towel to an ageing obese woman emerging from the surf at Bude. Underneath are the words:

It's time to take me home.

According to the magazine, you can purchase a bespoke mandroid like this one or an equivalent femdroid for just over two hundred pounds.

How illogically cheap, she thinks. It must cost more than twice as much to manufacture it.

She glances once more at the mandroid, then slaps the magazine back with the others, retrieves her bag, unlocks the door of her own consulting room and switches on the lights.

As she draws back the curtains, she pauses to watch a throng of swarthy birds in the trees in the park opposite. It's stupid but she imagines that over the weekend the rookery has been gradually edging closer to her surgery.

How absurd, she thinks. Rooks move. Rookeries do not.

But her heart races when she sees a huge spider grope its way over the long bench cushion under the bay window. She tries to be calm, even scientific.

Orange legs. Must be a false widow.

She had met worse creatures than this overseas. Scorpions especially – and deadly little vipers. Yet this *thing,* right here in England in her own surgery feels more threatening, like some loathsome intruder, totally alien.

The spider scuppers into the folds of the curtain only to reappear on top of the pelmet, where it squats back on its abdomen, raising its front legs like a drummer about to perform.

Connie grabs a white towel, climbs onto a chair, swipes the spider to the floor, then jumps down to crush it underfoot. Again and again she pulps the arachnid into the laminate, yet still it refuses to die, its spindly legs are splayed taut like the pointy fingers of a tiny demon, all broken but still flexing.

She shudders with revulsion as she sweeps the remains into a dust pan and shakes them out the window, then she soaks a corner of the towel in disinfectant and goes down on her hands and knees to wipe the mess off the floor.

She only straightens up when she hears raucous lamentations coming from the rookery.

Five

At Sherborne Station Harris jots down the arrival of a young man holding hands with a strikingly attractive brunette.

– drop-dead gorgeous – can't be human – must be a femdroid – does she need a train ticket?

But then the brunette turns her head from the man so he won't see her dabbing the point of her nose with a tissue.

– yes, that settles it – dabbing her nose makes her a real human being – but .... damn! I'm positive she really wants people to actually believe she's a femdroid. – I'm so chuffed – relieved really she's actually flesh and blood – when droids become like us – I find them so .... repellent.

He wonders if the two are married. Weddings are a sore point with Harris. He can't help brooding on one of his recent ceremonies at St Aethelthryrth's which was gate-crashed by about two hundred Stand Starers.

Despite the families and guests of the bride and groom doing all they could to keep the wedding a close secret right up to the actual day, social media prevailed and right on time the Stand Starers had turned up in cheaply hired buses for the 'Happening'.

There was nothing Harris could do about it because the Church had decreed that it was 'unacceptable' to turn them away.

The Prosecutor is incensed. 'Turn them away? As the celebrant priest you were supposed to have welcomed them as 'Our Surprise Guests'.

'Guests? Like hell they were.'

Harris remembers them standing like wax effigies of themselves during the whole wedding service. Most just fixed their dead fish eyes on Harris himself, others on the bride and groom.

A few had been still in the early stages of becoming Stand Starers and actually moved. Two came right up to the very steps of the altar. Others slouched up to individual members of the congregation who became so intimidated that they rushed out of the church to lock themselves in their cars.

Harris recalled one man with wild hair and filthy long nails, his clothes reeking of tobacco and stale sweat. He dragged himself up the steps to the pulpit, so close that Harris nearly choked on his stinking breath.

Any nearer and I swear I would've punched his lights out.

'And what would that have got you?' chides the Prosecutor.

'Satisfaction.'

'But what would Jesus have said?'

'Jesus would've understood.'

SHORTLISTED

EMILY HUGHES

Ghost Boy

Synopsis
The Valentines are a family in trouble, struggling to hold it together. Then one day twelve-year-old, autistic Rex starts seeing ghosts, and everything begins to unravel...

The burden of dealing with Rex's invisible disability is a weight felt keenly by each family member, both physically and emotionally. Suzy (mum) is overprotective of her son. Mike (dad) is largely absent, although he has an easy bond with Rex which Suzy envies. Mike and Suzy do not agree on how to deal with the increasingly challenging situations arising as a result of Rex's behaviour. Their relationship has become abrasive, wearing them both down.

Meanwhile, Rex must contend with a turmoil of emotions: the 'redrage' and the 'wild-jerky' frequently overwhelm him. Life for Rex is a living hell. His anxiety manifests as hostile behaviour, particularly towards ten-year-old Cherry. He escapes into his fantasy world where he can become 'Ghost Boy', disappear altogether.

One day a real ghost appears in Rex's bedroom. Rex believes that Sim is here to help him discover the source of the darkness he finds inside him, but he soon discovers Sim has his own darkness. After a series of events which climax with Mike leaving home and Rex getting into a fight at school, he runs away and is knocked down by a car.

Rex finds himself with Sim in a grey, liminal space. Meanwhile, Rex's family is slipping through the gaps of their own woven reality, consumed by guilt and fear as Rex lies in a coma. Whilst his family hangs by a thread, Rex must dig deep, fight his demons to escape this nightmare. Only then can the family begin to ground themselves back in their own realities, and move on.

Going Under
Suzy
The day you drowned is there, cauterised in memory. You always loved the water, ever since you were tiny. At bathtime you flapped and flapped

your caterpillar arms and legs in a frenzied fit of energy. A mechanical toy wound up too tight. Sometimes you flung your head back against the cradle of my arm with the force of a cannonball, froze yourself into a rigid cross, held in your breath. You loosened. Dark eyes fluttered, sunk to the back of your head. After that you would sleep for hours. You had these crazy little explosive moments, climax, release. The first time it happened, I thought you were dying.

When you were three months old I took you to the swimming pool with some mothers from my NCT group. Their babies were startled, wide-eyed, gradually adjusting to new sensations. But you wanted to torpedo yourself right under. You thrashed about like a fish out of water as if you were gasping to be back on land. The other mothers stood around bobbing their placid lumps about in their arms or wedged tightly against the ledges of their hips, waving colourful plastic toys and blowing raspberries in front of blinking faces. They watched me nervously, wrangling you, a slippery weight. A wayward force I couldn't quite control. They said they'd never seen a baby react like that before. They waded in closer, forming a tight circle around us. Mothers can smell panic in the air like a shark smells a single drop of blood dissolved in seawater. The possibility of disaster lives just under their skin, always close to the surface. They were tense, buoyant, holding in a concerted breath. After all it was hard to tell if you were enjoying it at first. If this was the usual state of affairs between us. But then you relaxed, suddenly compliant, all smiles and delighted yelps and giggles. The mothers parted and swished away slowly, exhaling wavering murmurs. Everyone was relieved, including me, so we all laughed a little bit too loudly. You were funny. A funny little thing. They cooed and clucked and smiled indulgent smiles. He loves it! Ah, bless. Look how much he loves it, Suze. Must be a natural. But you weren't a natural. As it turned out, you weren't a natural at anything.

When you were older, Mike and I took you to the sea. We had tried swimming lessons in groups, even one to one, but you ignored the instructions they shouted out at you, your senses submerged. I would come to pick you up and you would be sitting on the side, shivering, upset, confused. The instructor would give you a wary glance and pat you on the head. Important to stay safe, eh mate? Try harder next time? But there was never a next time. We took you swimming alone and you learned to navigate your way through the water well enough, even if your methods were unorthodox. You would swim whole lengths underwater, arms butterflying by your side, pulsing your legs up and down like a fin. You found your rhythm, and a grace you couldn't quite summon on land. But the sea was different to the swimming pool. It was endless for a start, the horizon as unreachable as a rainbow. You did not understand abstract things. You knew limits and boundaries and rails to grab hold of and they made you feel safe. Your understanding of the gravity of things was muddled, askew. The things that you loved the most were also the things that were the most frightening, overwhelming for you. I knew I could not keep you safe. I was scared for you.

We stood at the edge holding hands, the water flirting with our toes. You fidgeted next to me, swinging my arm back and forth until my joints uncoiled. I felt a crack in my shoulder. You squirmed your hot sweaty fingers in mine, corkscrewed them this way and that until you managed to work them free.

You were gone.

You surrendered yourself to the sea as I knew you would: arms open, eyes wide as the dead. You curled yourself up into a ball and let the salt buoy you and the gentle swishing currents toss you about, drift you further from me. I tracked your smooth, curved back, breaking the surface from time to time. I followed you, mining my body against the water, which felt thick as tar. My stomach clenched with cold. I wasn't a strong swimmer and I tired easily even though the water was calm. The salt stung at my skin and my eyes. Each time I reached out to grab your ankles you would laugh and kick me away in a flurry of bubbles which blinded me. You were deft, mercury-sleek. Tricky as a silverfish. Did you want to be gone? Did you want to disappear? For that thin, mutable line to swallow you up? I had to wonder. I couldn't hold my breath as long as you and when I surfaced, panting, you were nowhere to be seen.

For those few moments I was struck. I stumbled out of the water, punch drunk with grief, trying desperately to hold the fractured parts of me together. I dragged my sopping body out onto the sand and up the beach, clambering, my swimming costume pouched with seawater, tears burning fresh salt trails down my face.

There you were.

Mike had stripped you and was rubbing your goose-fleshed body up and down vigorously with a towel. There you were. Laughing at how you had managed to evade me. A fun game, to wind mummy up. There you were. You hadn't drowned. *You hadn't drowned.* But you had drowned. In those brief moments, you had, to me. I wanted to slap you, to shock you into contrition. Mike was laughing too. D'ya have fun buddy? he said and he looked at me and I stood, bending over, breathing hard, a little apart so he couldn't see that I was shaking. I rose up slowly, dripping, glowering.

We had only brought one towel. You're too overprotective, Suze! he mocked, moving towards me, attempting a playful punch on my arm. I scooped my body sideways and grabbed his fist in mine. I wanted to slap him too. He wrestled it free easily, shrugged. Should've let me go in with him. We could have had some fun, eh buddy? Doing shark dives? Mike pressed his palms together and motioned a swooping dive with his hands, made a silly face and you laughed again and threw off your towel and bounced about like a Mexican jumping bean, jabbering, teeth chattering.

Someone had to stay and look after Cherry! I shrieked.

The noise startled the seagulls. Several other people on the beach looked over towards us. The warm salt breeze was picking up, flicking my wet hair into my eyes, crystallising my anger. Mike was quiet and stopped his horseplay, but you carried on thumping your tiny feet into the coarse yellow sand. I looked over at Cherry. Thankfully she had slept through the whole thing in her pram. I knew the stinging truth was that I didn't trust Mike. I didn't trust him to be sensible, to keep a proper eye on you. I had once left you at the beach with him to go and buy ice creams. On my return, you had scaled a huge pile of jagged rocks and Mike had been standing at the bottom, cheering you on.

I saw the black jutting edges, slippery, sharp as knives. I saw you dancing on the summit, King of your mountain, the wet green slime under your bare feet, glistening in the sunshine.

I tried then, not to relive what could have happened if I hadn't dropped the ice creams and run over, climbed up the rocks and fetched you down myself. I tried not to, as I recalled that day, pushing the nagging thoughts to the back of my head.

Mike was sitting in front of me at the water's edge, his body hunched over, hands tracing sinking patterns into the wet sand. He looked so dejected, staring wistfully at you picking up fistfuls of pebbles and chucking them into the sea. Hips rippling, arms spinning in their sockets, laughing and launching catapults with abandon. But in an instant your mood switched and you were fussing and crying over the sand between your toes and Mike was there, perplexed, trying to brush it off and console you. I suddenly felt guilty that I had denied him a first experience with you, when he had already missed so many. Next time, I mumbled, more to myself than to him, since he was too far to hear anyway. I picked up the discarded towel and set off after you. You were whooping and streaking, stark naked, already half way down the beach.

When I finally caught up with you, you fell into my arms, shrieking, sent me flying. I tussled with your wet squirming body like a rugby player in a scrum. It was what I imagined it would be like trying to contain an octopus, or a giant squid.

Right from the beginning, I knew. There was something off-kilter about you. You were too yielding, too rigid. My plasticine prince. I felt it in the way you would crash into me, make a breaker of your magnificent weight, cushioning down your bowling ball head, crinoline limbs flapping. You were wide open to the world, never thinking to hold anything back. And somehow I knew that if I didn't stand in its way, make myself a buffer against the waves, then it would claim you for itself one day.

Over time, I became a palette of quiet, pounded shades. Your mother. Your protector. You surrendered yourself to me in the way only a true innocent can, with a kind of yawning nonchalance, hurling outrageous elliptic demands. You always expected, always knew: I would just be there, a brittle, slender turitella, waiting to be filled up by you.

* * *

The naming happened on the second September day. The first day — the day the thick slapping waves began to crash through my belly and down to my bowels — was a fickle one. We had all the weathers: bright sunshine, brisk wind, clattering hail, lashing rain. By late afternoon the sky was still and grey, tired of its exertions. It was the longest day of my life and you clung on to it. Waited it out. You were born right at the cusp: 11.59pm. One minute to midnight.

The thing about pregnancy is the weight it expounds in you. You grew, heavy as a fruit, inside me. And in those days when I was shining and ripe, you would beat me like a drum even then. Mould me with the jab of a heel or the furl of a fist into an awkward kind of sanctuary which I kept hard and taut as a pea pod. You erupted on a bloody screaming riptide. It heaved and hammered and pounded at me. I burst. Belched you out. A small waxy grub with dark gashes for eyes. They slapped you onto my chest, skin-to-skin, and straight away you tried to burrow your way back down into me. You clung to my midriff, curled up like a leach. You were still screaming. I reached out a hand to touch you: your tiny clenched fists, slick black head, warm puckered body. I had expected a cold, slimy thing.

You stopped screaming and I started. The pain racked up, walled up, closing in. There was a fuss and a scuffle and the doctor was called. I had a sudden premonition that something catastrophic was going to happen. But it had already happened.

Take it off me! I cried. I had birthed a monster which had ripped me apart with its relentless claws. And they did, they took you away and I wanted to crawl off into a corner in the way that animals do when they are ready to die. I wanted to be alone with my pain, to nurse it, to lick my wounds. But my body was not my own anymore and hadn't been for a long time.

The surgeon was a woman. I remember being grateful for that. She'll know what to do, I thought. She'll be sympathetic to how the anatomy should go down there. I can trust her. Her face told me it was going to be a tough job, but I didn't care. I submitted myself to her wholly and sighed with a deep shudder when I felt the sharp prick at the base of my spine. That euphoric tingle. Absolution. Drowning out the thumping, gaping emptiness. Finally, here was my moment of unfettering.

What are you going to call him? she asked, trying to make conversation whilst she worked. I marvelled that she could be so casual and light when dealing with such slaughter, such sombre butchery. When one wrong stitch could mean a hole closed too tight, a jagged edge to my soft folds down there. I imagined my cunt as a war zone, a sort of cubist farrago, Picasso's *Guernica*. I don't know, I replied. I had to stop myself from saying I didn't care in the least, that I didn't love you. Not yet. Well, at least he's healthy, she said, smiling, as if that excused this mess. You must be so happy. A good weight. Well done you!

Yes. Well done me. And all I could think was if this is supposed to be the happiest moment of my life, then something is very wrong.

But slowly, I would get used to that kind of talk, the you before me, and then gradually, eventually, being erased from the picture altogether. It wouldn't get easier, but after a while it wouldn't really matter so much anymore. And I would come to understand that learning to be a woman is about learning to fold up the pain into a neat pouch of blood-soaked wadding and tuck it away. Usually best to swallow, down the throat, larynx, trachea (try not to choke), bronchi, then deep down inside some fleshy pink lung pocket. Stuff it right in. But I didn't know that the baleful torrent on which you had emerged had also planted a seed of rage which would take up root and bloom into delicate red trees, blocking up my airways, so that there would be times when I would have to stop, bend over, unable to breathe.

Mike named you in the end. I didn't see the rush, but he said you didn't feel like ours until you had a name, not properly. He said you didn't seem real. He said it was a good strong name, the kind people wouldn't mess around with in silly diminutive forms. I know in his head, as he held you for those first hours, he was dreaming of fishing trips and football games in the park and bike rides and walks in the woods, teaching you about nature and all the names of all the things in the world around you. You could have been anything then. The possibility of you was something utterly wonderful, utterly terrifying. But even when you had your name, you never stopped being a fairytale to me.

Oh, I suffered the caprice of the gods that day. I was their plaything. Lying there on a hospital bed, sluiced and hooked up, hung up, blood drained, fibres slackened. Fat congealing to a waxy paste. You split me wide open. But then you split everything wide open. It was your way. And when I was done, skin hitched, hand-stitched, I became something else entirely. An emerging, newborn thing. Flailing, just like you.

To comply with our rules, Emily Hughes withdrew her novel from the competition while the shortlisted novels were being read as she was offered representation by an agent.

RUNNER-UP

SANDRA JENSEN

Seagull Pie

Synopsis
It's 1974. Samantha's father is dead. Her mother is a poverty-stricken sculptor and anti-apartheid activist. Samantha is twelve and hurtling into puberty, and her brother, Michael, is on the cusp of university. The family have been living in England since escaping South Africa (via Greece where Samantha's father was killed in a car accident), but England is in a recession and people are collecting butter vouchers not art. Catholic priest Father Murphy invites Beryl to start a craft centre in Ireland. Beryl is a resolute atheist but she takes up the Father's invitation, re-locating her family to the wilds of Donegal, bringing along her 80-year-old stone-deaf mother-in-law, Bonma and Samantha's Afghan hound, Natasha.

The family last one year in the schoolhouse, during which Beryl creates Father Murphy's craft centre and attempts to keep her family happy and self-sufficient. The results are disastrous. Their crops are finished off by the neighbouring farmer's sheep, a badger massacres the chickens and the villagers avoid the craft centre as if it were frequented by the Devil himself.

For Christmas Samantha concocts a seagull pie, made from a seagull her brother fells with a slingshot. Bonma has a stroke while eating her pie, waking up in a hallucinatory world in which she waits for Johnny Noo-Noos and the Ding Dongs to arrive in their rocketship and whisk her away to a good life of parties in London.

Things go from bad to worse when a neighbouring cottage is frequented by the IRA, Michael starts growing marijuana and Bonma flings bricks through the schoolhouse windows believing Beryl to be abducted by an 'evil sister'. The car is packed up and Beryl drives the family to Belfast, anticipating a relative haven of culture and sensibility. In fact, 1975 is one of the bloodiest years of 'The Troubles'.

Seagull Pie
'Glencolumbkille. How do you even say that?' I try out different ways of pronouncing it. Mum needs help to keep her awake. It's four in the

morning and we've been waiting hours in line for the Stranraer to Larne ferry. The car stinks of exhaust fumes from the other cars waiting. It stinks of Bonma's perfumy face powder and my lapful of hairy dog, digestive biscuit crumbs, crisp packets and my greasy hair. We are all grumpy after driving twelve hours to get here. It would have been less if Bonma hadn't needed to stop every twenty minutes to pee or eat or complain. And if I hadn't told Mum to take the wrong exit at the roundabout near Doncaster. My brother Michael has gone ahead with the moving van so I'm the designated map reader. Mum's the driver and Bonma's, well, I don't know. She's my grandmother but I wish she wasn't. We've been lumped with her ever since the car accident which brought quite a few things to an abrupt end. My father being one of them. I can't say *Dad* because he wouldn't let us call him that, and saying his real name, *Tony*, just makes my ears echo, as if the word is trying to find something to stick to.

I've spilled Ribena on my yellow-and-black top I crocheted that was supposed to look like a bee but looks like a dartboard. It now looks like there's blood on it. I rub at the stain. It's on my right bosom. It hurts a bit to rub, and I feel that sick, draggy feeling in my stomach. I've stuffed a wad of toilet paper in my panties just in case my period is coming. I haven't been keeping track. I don't want to know. I don't want anyone to know. I don't think anyone does but Mum has recently been hovering near the tampon and sanitary aisle waving her arm in an obscure direction, saying, 'Do you need anything, Darling?' She slows down at the underwear section too and turns her head vaguely at the bras. That's when I go off and say, 'We're out of Cornflakes.' I hate her. I hate my breasts. They are a weird shape and my nipples are all wrong. I tried on Mum's bras when she was at work. She's a 34B. I'm not yet. She's got some white ones from Marks and Sparks, but the ones I like are from when we lived in South Africa, little pink satin panty and bra sets with white lace around the edges and a black bra that has pads in the cups to push you up and together so there's cleavage and tiny red bows. I love this bra so much it hurts my throat.

I go back to saying Glencolumbkille. I try it out backwards, 'Ellikbmulocnelg,' and Mum laughs.

Bonma says, 'THIS IS NOT A LAUGHING MATTER, BERYL ELIZABETH,' in her foghorn voice that I've inherited. She's got lipstick on her teeth and I'm not going to point it out, or rather, write it out because she's stone deaf and that is what we do, write everything down for her. Little bits of paper covered in our various scrawls littered our house in Somerset. Margins of newspapers crammed with information. *She's having an affair with Duke. Yes he's married. To the blonde woman. Yes the big breasted blonde woman.* I'm the self-appointed explainer of what's on TV because Michael and Mum just ignore her endless questions. Bonma watches Coronation Street, Fred Astaire musicals, Carry On films and anything with sex in it, like I Claudius. When people kiss or grope each other she says, 'THAT'S DISGUSTING!' and keeps watching, cigarette stuck to her lip and dripping ash onto Mum's Kilim rug.

'I STILL DON'T UNDERSTAND WHY WE ARE LEAVING GREAT BRITAIN,' Bonma says.

I flick through my writing pad for where I told her before: *Because an Irish priest saw that BBC special and thinks God was sending him a message to ask a famous South African sculptor to start his craft centre in middle-of-nowhere Donegal.*

'I READ THAT ALREADY. IT EXPLAINS NOTHING.'

'Finally,' Mum says as we drive slowly into the dark hole of the ferry.

We can't find the way to the dog kennels so we go to the foyer. It's packed with people milling about looking for their cabin. We don't have money for cabins which disappoints me greatly. I remind myself Bonma would have been with us in the cabin. The foyer has a red carpet and a plastic chandelier and a bulbous-faced ferry steward in a white and gold uniform. Natasha keeps winding her lead around my legs and whimpering.

Mum makes her way through the crowd to the desk and a man steps aside for her and looks down her shirt. 'You 'n me,' he says, 'you 'n me.' He's winking and pushing a piece of paper at her which I assume has his cabin number on.

My mother says, 'For Christ's sake,' and dings the bell.

Margaret – I call Bonma Margaret when I don't want anyone to know she's my grandmother – taps ash onto the carpet and says, 'WHERE'S MY CABIN, BERYL ELIZABETH, SHOW ME TO MY CABIN,' and I fish out my writing pad to tell her we don't have one but that's when Natasha hunches her back and fixes me with her sweet almond eyes. She's having a poo.

She's got diarreah so it makes a wet noise and the crowd pulls away from her so she's right there, in the middle of the floor with a big space around her making a drippy heap on the red carpet and everyone is pointing and I'm trying to pretend it's not my dog but that's hard when she's on the end of the lead I'm holding.

Mum elbows her way towards me. I wish she wouldn't because it's just making everything more obvious and I'm so hot in the face it feels like my pimples will explode all over the crowd.

Seagull Pie

'YOU'VE STEPPED IN IT BERYL ELIZABETH,' Margaret says.

The ferry steward pulls out his walkie-talkie and pushes it against his face shouting, 'B3 to C4, B3 to C4!'

I'm a swish of open mouths with wet lips and teeth and tongues like bits of meat all yawing at me pointing and laughing *ha ha ha* and the bulbous-faced steward yelling into his walkie-talkie, 'That's not my remit, that's not my bloody remit you come down here right now.'

My mother has Margaret by the elbow but she's having none of it. 'LOOK AT YOUR SHOE, BERYL ELIZABETH,' she says and everyone looks at my mother's shoe which is a deep treaded trainer she found at Oxfam trying to get me in there to buy shoes for school but that's where Bonma buys all her shoes. She's got forty-seven pairs. We counted.

The next thing I know we are upstairs. I'm sitting at a Formica-topped table with my mother who is furiously smoking her cigarette. Bonma is slumped forward and would be face-first on the Formica if her bosoms weren't in the way. The table is littered with biscuit wrappers and plates smeared with grease and egg so I suspect we've eaten something.

I suddenly feel like throwing up but can't get out because Bonma is blocking my way.

'Mum,' I say, 'Mum,' but she just looks out the window at the black outside and the rain smashing.

'Weather, eh,' says the man who'd said, *You 'n me, you 'n me*. He's found us or rather found my mother, who just keeps staring at the black. He lurches off looking depressed.

I try to keep my eyes away from the plates of grease and egg. The restaurant is full of drunk people. I smell vomit but it's not mine. It's the woman at the table behind who's thrown up onto her own Formica table. She doesn't seem concerned, she just stares at it. The bulbous-faced steward lumbers past with his walkie-talkie but he doesn't seem concerned either. I wonder why Natasha's poo is so much worse than this woman's vomit which is dribbling onto the floor because the ship's tipping sideways. The steward is at the bar ordering Guinness. That doesn't seem right but he's got two in his hands as he comes back past, his walkie-talkie stuffed into his trousers, someone's scratchy voice coming from it saying, 'C4 to B3? C4 to B3?'

I feel uncomfortably wet in my crotch and I remember the wad of toilet paper there. My jeans are black so even if there was a leakage problem it would be OK, but I climb over Bonma to find the Ladies. I latch the cubicle door. The wad is soaked with blood. It smells like the tin roof we had on our house in Johannesburg. We'd dry apricots in the sun on that roof. I try to flush the wad down the toilet but it clogs and water starts to rise to the top and begins to leak down the sides. There's no plunger. I can't step out because there are people out there and they'd see. I close my nose and put my hand in the pink water to try and dislodge the wad. Bits of brown and yellow and a flake of lettuce speckle the sides of the toilet. Tears rush up the back of my nose and out my eyes and I can't stop myself from retching.

'You alright in there?' someone says, knocking on the door. I can see her shoes, pointy silver sandals with heels and her toes sticking out. Sad toes crossing over each other with chipped glitter nail polish. I wonder how she can wear sandals in winter.

She knocks again. 'Are you alright? Don't drown or anything.'

Another woman titters so I don't open the door. I'm never going to open the door. I'm going to stay here until she goes away with my hand covered in my period and toilet water. I try to sniff my snot silently which makes my head smart. I fashion another sanitary pad from the roll of toilet paper and stuff it into my panties trying not to touch too much of me with the hand that went down the toilet. The water is slowly subsiding. There's a bottle of bleach but no brush. I pour it in anyway. I lower the seat, hold my hand far away from me and wait for the cross-toed woman and her friends to leave. I think they have and I unlatch the door when I hear, 'IS THIS THE LADIES?'

I latch it back. I think about pouring bleach on my disgusting hand. The ship rocks violently and Bonma says, '**THIS IS WORSE THAN THE STEAMER FROM CAPE TOWN TO ATHENS.**'

FIRST PRIZE

GEORGE KELLY

City of Blades

Synopsis
City of Blades *traces the struggle of a young teen, Deante, and his fight for freedom. With both parents dead—his mum succumbing to the needle, his dad to the gang life—Deante spends his days waiting hand and foot on his older brother and legal guardian, Andre West. Deante simply wants to study and create funny YouTube videos, but his brother is adamant he 'man-up' and get involved with Andre's violent gang, The Real Talks Crew, or suffer his wrath. His brother's building an army and is in the early stages of plotting a coup of the South London drug and prostitution trade, and wants Deante by his side.*

Deante fights to keep his innocence as much as he can, until he discovers his older sister's missing, possibly kidnapped by a rival gang, and no one seems to care.

With the help of his school friend and love interest, Hannah Evans, Deante has to confront everything he's been running from in order to save his sister and escape his brother.

He has to learn to live by the blade . . . or die by it.

> *'Nobody can give you freedom.*
> *Nobody can give you equality or justice or anything.*
> *If you're a man, you take it.'* — **Malcolm X**

Chapter 1: Blow His Brains Out
THE TROUBLE STARTED SOON AFTER Andre's friends showed up.
　Deante had been in his room playing the new FIFA on his PS4, glad to be off the clock for the night—food cooked, house cleaned, chores completed. But then Andre's friends arrived, and his brother ordered him into the living room to socialise.
　'And fix your face,' Andre said. 'You look miserable.'
　Deante parked up on the sofa and leaned forward, keeping his focus on the TV on the wall, a 60-inch Sony. The music channel was playing in silence: an endless parade of half-naked thick-thighed Insta girls, intercut

with an occasional shot of a miming rapper, with face tattoos and multi-coloured hair, his neck draped in oversized chains. Without the sound it seemed kind of comical, this big-time gangster awkwardly waving his hands around, looking more like a puppet on a stage than a hardened career criminal.

On the sofa to Deante's right, Andre billed up a spliff, his third of the evening.

To his left, Andre's two friends were slouched on the settee, one on each side of a light-skinned girl, vying for her attention. One of them, a dark-skinned guy called Marlon, showed her pictures of a recent night out, swiping across on his iPhone, probably showing her a reel of typical hood shots: him at the bar holding an expensive bottle of *Cristal* champagne, or him sat in VIP with a wad of fifties conveniently laid out on the table in front. If Deante's sister Candice was here, they'd be huddled together in the corner, quietly mocking him, laughing at how pathetic he was. But she was in her room making plans with the devil, most likely with a plastic tube twisted around her upper arm and a needle full of juice at her side.

'Bruv,' he said to Andre, 'can I go to bed? It's late . . .'

'Nah.' Andre finished rolling his spliff and sparked it up. He took a couple puffs, then handed it over to Deante. 'I want you here. Take a hit.'

'I'm cool.'

'Oi, take a hit, man.'

'I'm good, bruv.'

'Listen—' Andre said, holding up the spliff. 'Don't fuckin' embarrass me.'

The look in his eyes was hard, a concrete surface, and Deante knew what lay behind it: promises of a beating if he disobeyed Andre in front of his friends. His brother spent at least two hours a day exercising, usually in his room pumping free weights—and he stood tall at 6'3, a reinforced unit with tight, lean muscles. In contrast, Deante was 5'11 at best and built for hugs. A few weeks back Andre punched him in the thigh to give him a dead leg, and he'd limped for almost a fortnight. Andre could probably punch through a titanium door.

'A'ight,' Deante said, and took the spliff. He sucked in the smoke, the end flaring like a beacon, and coughed it out. '*Rah*. That's proper strong, man.'

'Take a few more,' he said. 'Get yourself used to it.'

Deante had never been a fan of the stuff; it made his mouth taste funny. And now, after four or five more hits, his brain felt foggy too. The girl between Andre's friends looked like an Egyptian goddess floating in smoke. She seemed to be in her own world, ignoring the two horndogs next to her, instead scanning the framed blown-up photos around the room with no real interest: a *Scarface* poster, a few gangster rappers, a picture of a capsized boat washed-up on a beach, nothing memorable or interesting. Nothing relating to their family.

'Oi, Sherese,' Andre called out. 'Come 'ere, man, come sit.'

'What—right now, yeah?'

'Nah, tomorrow innit. Why don't you come here next fuckin' week?'

Sherese laughed and stood up, using the boys' knees to help her. She walked over on four-inch heels, wearing a gold piece of cloth that could barely be considered a skirt. Her V-neck top displayed a bulging cleavage. She sat on Andre's lap, draping her arm around his neck, and stroked the scar by his eye: a sickle-shaped mess of hard pink flesh that ran from his temple down to his lower jaw. 'You want me to dance for you, babes?'

'Nah. I want you to suck my bruvva's dick.'

'What?' She paused. 'Hold up, you being serious?'

'Of course.'

'How old is he?'

'Fifteen tomorrow. This is a lickle birthday present.'

'Yeah but—fifteen? Ain't that a bit young, Andre?'

'It's the perfect age for a man's first blowie.' He glanced at Deante, showing him hard eyes again: dark, hiding flames. 'He ain't never had no girl suck on him before, ain't that right Dee?'

His cheeks grew hot. 'Nah,' he mumbled.

'So there you have it,' Andre said. 'Man needs to pop that cherry, ya get me?'

One of Andre's friends, the lighter-skinned one, Terrik somebody, laughed, a high squeal that scraped through Deante's skull and echoed in his ears. The room seemed smaller, more suffocating, as if the walls had crept forward in the past five minutes. He wanted to run away.

Andre grinned at the girl. 'Go suck his dick.'

'But . . .' Sherese faltered. 'If he's only fifteen, ain't that seen as rape?'

'Nah, what's seen as rape,' Andre growled, gripping her by the neck, 'is if I tied you up to a radiator and brutalised your pussy, *that's* rape. Yeah? Ya understand?' He gripped her neck harder and she let out a small shriek. 'You don't like that, do you?'

'No.'

'Right.' His voice low, menacing. 'Do you want me to hurt you?'

'No,' she said weakly.

'Then don't disrespect me in front of company.'

'I'm sorry.'

'A'ight, good,' he said, letting go. 'Now go suck his dick. No more questions.'

'It's cool,' Deante said. 'She don't need to.'

'Shut up.'

'Nah, but it's cool though, bruv—' Deante not wanting his dick sucked anyway. He'd rather be in his room, reading a graphic novel or playing FIFA. Right now he'd pick anywhere else in the world: *Disneyland* or a torture chamber, it didn't matter which, just so long as he could leave this situation and pretend it never happened. He imagined how he'd feel if his sister Candice was forced into the same position and the thought sent anger crashing through his body. But it was a weak, impotent feeling. What exactly could he do? Andre would smash his head through a brick wall.

'Sherese,' Andre said, 'I'm not playin'. Go suck his dick.'

'Can I take her to my room?' he asked, hoping he could pre*tend* she gave him head, just walk out the door in ten minutes belting up his jeans and looking satisfied.

'Nah.' Andre pushed Sherese into his lap. 'Hurry up, man, you're takin' long.'

Andre's other friend, Marlon, said: 'I don't think she wants to do it G.'

'I didn't ask you,' Andre said.

'Yeah,' Terrik said.'Let the girl eat a dick.'

'Go ahead,' Andre said to Sherese. 'We ain't got all day.'

Reluctantly, Sherese hunched over and slowly unbuckled his belt, Deante fighting the nausea rolling through him. This wasn't his idea of sexy. This wasn't how he planned to have his first sexual experience, in a room full of degenerates, laughing and smoking weed whilst a girl was forced to pleasure him. Tears were building behind his eyes but he held them back, knowing that showing weakness could lead to something much worse.

Sherese wrapped her hand around his shrivelled cock, her fingers warm but her rings cold against his skin. A whimper escaped her throat, something Andre and his friend Terrik found hilarious, their laughter bouncing through his head. He looked off at the wall, not wanting to maintain eye contact with anyone, shame and embarrassment burning inside of him, like boiling hot oil in his bloodstream. He closed his eyes, shutting it all out. Then she put his cock in her mouth and began to suck it—and despite his desire to not be a part of this, his dick grew hard, his body complicit in an act he didn't want to take place.

Terrik laughed again, that high-pitched squeal. 'Yes-yes G, break her *throat*, nig-gaaaaa,' he sang out. Andre's other friend, Marlon, looked off to the side, unimpressed.

And with each thrust of Sherese's head, her mouth sliding up and down, a pulse throbbed in Deante's throat. It might have been guilt, or maybe even pleasure, he wasn't sure. Either way, he wanted it to stop; wanted to blink and wake up elsewhere, anywhere.

Eventually he said, 'I'm not gonna cum, bruv,' which was the truth. How could he? His mind was in a hundred different places. His dick was hard but his brain limp, sexual thoughts lost in the depravity of it all. Andre told Sherese she was done and Deante quickly zipped himself up and went to the bathroom to clean up. After closing the door, he slid down it and slowly broke into tears, letting out all that tension in one go, huge galvanising shivers racking through his body. He cried into his T-shirt, keeping the sound to a minimum as he sobbed. He was back to being a child again, watching his mother shoot up and begging her to stop. He washed his face twice to hide the truth of his tears, and nobody appeared to notice his red eyes when he returned to the room.

They *all* had red eyes.

Marijuana eyes.

Sherese was back between Andre's friends, looking at the framed photos again, disconnected from the room, as if searching for an escape route, a way to forget about everything. He wanted to go over there and hug her, tell her he was sorry and comfort her in some small but insignificant way. But Andre would break him into pieces if he tried.

Instead, he said, 'Can I go to my room now?'

Andre barely looked at him. 'Yeah, fuck off to bed. It's late now anyway.'

* * *

ON THE MORNING OF HIS fifteenth birthday, Deante headed to his sister's room.

It was early, just after 8, but he wanted to talk to her about last night. He could still picture the look of fear in the girl's eyes as she was forced to give him head in a room full of hyenas. He should have stood up to his brother, refused to let the girl near him. But instead he'd allowed it to happen and now he didn't know how to take it back.

He just wanted Candice to tell him it wasn't his fault.

On her door, an old handwritten sign read KEEP OUT!!! in block letters. Below it, a worn sticker: INTRUDERS WILL BE PROSECUTED, a remnant from her teen years. She was almost 22 now, and she hadn't thought, or couldn't be bothered, to change it to something else or peel the stickers off completely.

Gently, he knocked on the door.

Twenty seconds ticked by but she didn't answer, so he knocked again.

Then he clutched the handle to enter, and stopped. He'd learned long ago not to enter rooms if he didn't know what he'd find; first with his mum, then with Andre for different reasons. The last time he saw Candice she'd been slumped at the kitchen table—track marks like cigarette burns on the insides of her brown arms, a pool of chunky vomit staining the floor by her feet, which she'd made no attempt to wipe up. She was lucky Deante saw her first and cleaned her up, helped her back into bed. If Andre had found her, he probably would have taken a belt to her arms and back, whipping her until thick welts rose all over her flesh. They'd only spoken about her addiction once, and Andre made his feelings clear: *Your sister's weak and useless, just like our mum was.*

He knocked a final time, just in case.

Still no answer.

Sleeping, most likely. Hugging up to the heroin of her dreamworld.

He'd try again later.

After a quick shower and breakfast, he got dressed and headed to school.

On his way he stopped in a card shop and bought himself a birthday badge. Not a big one, nothing extravagant that would stand out or flash or sing a song or anything. Just a small one, a blue fifteen badge that he pinned to his top so people would know it was his birthday. Otherwise, how could they tell? He didn't *look* any older. He didn't feel it, either. Fifteen years old and he couldn't tell the difference from when he was eleven. His eyes were the same shade of mahogany brown, and his skin remained dark and smooth, although wisps of hair were pushing through on his cheeks and his top lip, which was something at least. And his afro was growing larger too. He'd been letting it get wilder and wilder, knowing eventually one of the girls at school would offer to braid it. They'd invite him around to their house to plait it and then maybe he'd catch a kiss or even a feel-up from it. If he was lucky, Hannah Evans from his English class would be the first to offer. Or he'd approach her, put it to her straight: *Can you plait my hair?* But in the meantime he kept it tied in a small ponytail—using two black bands he'd taken from his sister's room—leaving him with a puff of hair at the back. He kind of liked it this way.

When he arrived at school, ten minutes early, he headed straight for his locker and punched in 18-10-60 to open it, his mother's birthdate. As he grabbed some revision material, he thought of his mum not being here, on his fifteenth birthday, dead from too much juice in her veins, and it poked him in the heart. Every year his mother used to make him a birthday card with hand-drawn cartoon characters on the front, and a long rambling message inside about how much she loved him, scrawled in her fancy handwriting. He still had them saved in a box at home. She also used to make him a cake too, chocolate with a Nutella filling. But now she was gone, dead and buried, and it seemed like Candice was heading in the same direction as her, following in her cracked infected footsteps. Deante couldn't let that happen. But what could he do to stop it?

Call the police? Get her dragged off to rehab?

He didn't trust any of them: the police, the doctors, none of them.

After their mother died, social services barely did anything to help him. As soon as they found out Andre had inherited the property with the mortgage paid, the social passed Deante into his care without a second thought. They arranged a follow-up meeting three months down the line to see how everything was going, but that was it. His mother was wiped off the planet with a self-inflicted overdose and these people popped their head through the door for two minutes like they were checking on an old acquaintance. Then it was: *bye, see ya Deante, have a nice life with your psychotic violent brother and your heroin addict of a sister.* At no point did any of them think to pull him aside, away from Andre, maybe ask how he was *really* doing, or if he needed help adjusting. It was merely a courtesy call—just something to tick off their to-do list as they carried on with their lives.

And if he stuck Candice in a clinic somehow, two weeks from now she'd be back on the streets, no better off, with a black mark by her name. He couldn't do that to her.

The thing is, he missed her. He missed their old relationship. Whereas his mother used to make him cards, Candice was always the first to wake him on his birthday, sitting at the end of his bed with a wrapped-up pile of graphic novels—and every time he used to hold up the present, knowing what was inside, and say something like 'Hmm, is it socks?' and they'd laugh. But not today. He figured she was too far hung up on the drugs to get him a present this year. Or maybe she'd forgotten it was his birthday altogether, or just didn't give a shit. That was the frightening part: what if she really didn't care anymore? Not only about Deante, but about life, or a family? What if she'd given up?

He didn't want to think about it. He closed his locker and turned back to the hall, nodding at a few people. Nobody said happy birthday, or appeared to notice his badge.

At the end of the hall he spotted Hannah Evans by her locker, the girl from his English class, and he stared at her, caught in her web, unable to function properly. She had that effect on him, like a magnet. Sometimes he'd spend an hour or more thinking about her hair, or the dimple in her cheek; not two like most people, just one, dipping in on the left side whenever she smiled or laughed. In *his* world, she was as large and bright as the sun. In her world, he was probably no more significant than a piece of gravel.

She closed her locker and walked down the hall in his direction.

His heart paused and he kept staring.

He didn't know how to move.

Oh shit.

Then she glanced at his badge and said, 'Happy birthday,' and drifted past him, like dropping a penny into a beggar's cup. He wasn't sure whether he replied or not.

All he could think was: I FUCKING LOVE YOU.

WENYAN LU

The Martyr's Hymn

Synopsis
The Martyr's Hymn *is a historical novel inspired by Lei Feng, a politically driven soldier in Red China. He died in a jeep accident in 1962 and was posthumously honoured as a martyr by Chairman Mao. The novel is narrated by Zhu Ansheng, the driver of the jeep in the fatal accident:*

Before Lei Feng's death
An orphan, Lei regards the Party as his surrogate mother. He displays his devotion to Chairman Mao and the Party by doing good deeds.

Lei is active in the collaborative frugality initiative between Shenyang Military Base and the central government in Beijing. Zhu works as his assistant.

Lei teaches Zhu Chairman Mao quotes.

After Lei Feng's death
Chairman Mao initiates the Learn from Lei Feng Movement, and Zhu becomes the official promoter of Lei Feng's spirit.

Zhu marries Meiliang, a primary teacher who has worked with Lei; they move to a remote farm.

During the denunciations of the Cultural Revolution (1966–1976), Zhu volunteers to go to prison to save the farm from political trouble.

In the post-Mao era, Zhu is called to promote Lei Feng's spirit again, together with Lei Feng's photographer Zhang Hua.

Meiliang dies of cancer.

Zhang has a heart attack and dies at the lectern on the 50th anniversary of the advent of the Learn from Lei Feng Movement.

Zhu mourns his youth and longs to be reunited with Lei Feng, Meiliang and Zhang Hua.

The novel brings to life the political slogans and quotes of Chairman Mao that characterize the times, and the absurdity of which contrasts with the seriousness of the theme.

The work explores the ways one's behaviour could be affected by the political context and how people's individual identity can be supressed, with their self-esteem largely determined by their loyalty to authority.

The Martyr's Hymn
Prologue

The Unheroic Death of a Hero, 15th August, 1962

I am a murderer.

I killed our nation's moral icon, Lei Feng.

It all happened fifty years ago.

It was a tragic waste. Lei Feng died in an accident – a mundane accident caused by me – such an unfitting death. If Lei Feng had lost his life while rescuing a drowning child from a swollen river, his sacrifice would have been more glorious.

How could the people of China bear their beloved hero dying so unheroically?

Several biographies were published shortly after Lei Feng's death. In those books, without exception I was described as the careless killer of a legend. No, they didn't say it in so many words, but reading between the lines, I was the one to blame – and I wouldn't disagree.

In one book, I was bursting with anguish: 'Zhu Ansheng exhibited symptoms of extreme guilt over his recklessness – he didn't check everything carefully before he reversed the jeep. At Lei Feng's funeral, Zhu threw himself onto the coffin and cried until he collapsed.'

In another book, I was silent: 'Zhu Ansheng couldn't clarify whether Lei Feng was hit by the jeep or the lamppost. The failure to confirm this piece of information left the details shrouded in mystery.'

I was also traumatised: 'Zhu Ansheng is known as Lei Feng's follower, which has made life without Lei Feng extremely hard for him. Rumour has it that his mental state is not stable.'

* * *

I was given free copies of those books, and I read each of them in tears.

There were some mistakes though: I did check everything before I reversed the jeep – in fact, I was directed by Lei Feng, I didn't go to the funeral and there was no coffin – he was lying on a ping pong table and my mental state was fine…

I thought it would be the end of me when I was called to be spoken to by a commander from the headquarters of Shenyang Military Base.

I was shaking when I entered the room, but the commander chatted to me as if nothing had happened.

Instead of being punished, I was assigned a mission.

Chapter One

The 50th Anniversary of Lei Feng's Death

By the side of my pillow lay an ancient shoe box containing Lei Feng's belongings. Some items had been replaced by replicas over the years, but nobody would know.

I ran my fingers over the medals on my military uniform. I didn't receive them for fighting in a war like a real soldier – instead, I was granted several heroic titles after I killed our own hero.

For 50 years, on and off, I had been telling Lei Feng's stories to audiences around the country. To make my stories go down better, sometimes I couldn't help changing details. I felt a little guilty at first, then I thought – well, I was spreading Lei Feng's spirit, so the content of the stories weren't that important.

I had a firm belief: whatever happened in this world, Lei Feng's spirit would never become dated – a good heart, revolutionary dedication and – above all – unswerving loyalty to our great leader, Chairman Mao, and our dear Party.

I wasn't sure whether I wanted to go to the ceremony to mark the death of a national hero (or rather, to mark *my killing* of a national hero – or even to mark my creation of a martyr). Was I too old to be among the crowds? On several occasions, I had overheard people saying I had dementia. I didn't mind hearing that – my 'dementia' would provide an excuse for me if anything went wrong.

I might not have dementia, but my health was naturally going downhill. In the last few years, I'd been feeling disoriented from time to time. I could barely stand the booming noise and the fervent atmosphere.

I was on my way out …

The script of the 50th anniversary talk had arrived in the post the week before. Years back, I'd been asked to set up an email account so I could communicate with people more effectively. I didn't know how, as I didn't have a computer, and I didn't want to have one either. I couldn't see the point – I didn't want to keep in touch with anyone, but it seemed people wanted to contact me.

As an authority on Lei Feng, I didn't need to be provided with scripts, but they were useful. They highlighted how many years Lei Feng had been dead, and who our current political leaders were – we were able to live in a safe, peaceful and prosperous society due to our leaders' wise and correct direction.

The 50th anniversary talk should start like this:

Dear Comrades and Friends,

I feel extremely honoured to be invited to talk to you about my dear brotherly comrade and esteemed moral icon, Lei Feng. Even though he has been away from us for fifty years, he has never really been absent. His spirit has always raised us up to the sublime.

Although we are living in the 21st century, we shall still value Lei Feng's qualities – kindness, thrift, selflessness and, most importantly, his loyalty to Chairman Mao and the Party.

You must have heard Lei Feng's stories before – everyone in this country has – but please allow me to show some of his belongings to you, and I will tell you the stories behind them, then you will have an idea of why we should admire him and remember him forever ...

I opened the shoe box, my treasure box: a copy of Chairman Mao's *Little Red Book*, a dog-eared yellowed diary, a badge of Chairman Mao, some black and white photos, a Swiss watch, a pair of patched odd socks and several bits and pieces of stationery.

The *Little Red Book* was in fact mine. It was a little red book with the grand official title *The Collected Thoughts of Chairman Mao,* which was published nearly two years after Lei Feng's death. Lei Feng did not live to see its publication, which I considered an intolerable shame and could not get over for several years.

Chairman Mao quotes had been studied in China ever since the Liberation in 1949. Lei Feng used to underline the quotes in thick volumes of Chairman Mao's thoughts and learnt them by heart. He had also helped many people understand and analyse them. It had been such a clever idea to publish a pocket book with the best quotes, allowing the people of China to study Chairman Mao's thoughts wherever they were.

I sometimes saw Lei Feng in my head waving the little red book with a genuine smile. He would no doubt have been set up as a pacemaker for the study of the *Little Red Book.*

As for the Swiss watch, it seemed nobody was convinced it had belonged to Lei Feng – being a frugal revolutionary Party member, he wouldn't have owned something so bourgeois. Although at first I insisted that I had seen him wearing the watch, I now doubted my memory...

I took out the *Little Red Book* and flicked through the pages – I would choose one or two quotes for the talks, usually when I realised not many people were concentrating. Without fail, the quotes would make people laugh – sometimes they even cheered.

My all-time favourite quote was:

The Martyr's Hymn

Revolution is not an invitation to a dinner party, is not writing essays, is not drawing or embroidery, cannot be that delicate, cannot be that calm or elegant, cannot be that gentle or humble; revolution is riots, a violent activity of one class overthrowing another.

The reason why I admired the quote so much was because it would always cause a stir, and people kept asking me if Chairman Mao had really said it. I would proudly show them the official publication code on the *Little Red Book* and the audience would be excited about the quote's authenticity. They thought Chairman Mao was funny; I had to correct them – Chairman Mao was wise, and one should never use the word *funny* when referring to our greatest leader.

There were other extraordinary quotes:
All our enemies are paper tigers.
If you can win, fight; if you cannot win, run away.
Our government's duty is to be responsible for its people.
And this one was a reflection of Lei Feng:
It is not difficult to do good deeds, but it is difficult to do good deeds all one's life.
I had been tempted to use this one, but I had never understood it:
The potatoes have been boiled, and some beef should be added. You do not need to fart, just watch how the world is turning upside down.
I shut the little red book.
I read the invitation again:

Dear respected Grandfather Zhu,
We are writing to invite you to join our new Learn from Lei Feng Movement in Shenyang. Your talk will form a major part of the activities on the day. To complement your talk, we have arranged some volunteers to offer free hairdressing to the public; some civil servants will sweep the pavements in the city centre; groups of university students will be sent to busy areas to help the old and the young and the infirm cross the road; around thirty primary and secondary school students who have achieved the highest grades in their end-of-year exams have been accorded the glory of paying a visit to Lei Feng's regimental dormitory. This year there is a new addition – the Bank of China is offering one-step bank card application; we believe this will attract many applicants, hence your audience will hopefully be greater than we originally planned. How exciting.
We have learnt that you have not given any formal talks for a year or two, due to your deteriorating health. We appreciate the situation, but we

believe you will consider participating because our initiative is to mark the 50th anniversary of Lei Feng's martyrdom and sacrifice to the building of our social and communal enterprise. We know how much he means to you.

There is also a poignant and precious fact we would like you to draw attention to: you are now the sole surviving close comrade of Lei Feng. You are the only person who can tell us about a genuine communist soldier, Chairman Mao's Good Pupil Lei Feng.

Special arrangements have been made to accommodate your physical needs. Two Party members will look after you at the venue and we have cancelled the question and answer session to avoid overtaxing you. Air-conditioning will be strictly controlled at an ethical temperature. We will manage time precisely to make sure you do not waste your time waiting. Every painstaking effort will be made to ensure your convenience and comfort.

Imagine how inspired the whole audience will be. Listening to a live talk by Lei Feng's comrade is a once-in-a-lifetime experience.

We need your collaboration to fight the increasing materialism amongst the youth, our nation's future – **they are the sun at about eight or nine o'clock in the morning**, *according to the words of Chairman Mao.*

Letters similar to this had been posted to me over the years. I started out as *Dear Big Brother Zhu*, then I became *Dear Uncle Zhu,* and now I had been a respected grandfather for the last decade. A *poignant* and *precious* fact – it was poignant that I would probably die soon and it was precious that someone who might soon be dead was still able to tell stories.

I wasn't upset at all – I had already outlived Lei Feng, a national hero, by fifty years. What else could I have asked for?

I wasn't left on my own though – I still had one close comrade who was actively alive.

I put on my uniform and stood in front of the mirror. I did look old, but I stood tall like a young soldier.

I would go. I would never miss a date with Lei Feng.
I felt I was approaching him, wherever he was.

Chapter Two

I Collapse at the Lectern

When I opened my eyes, I found myself lying on a bed. I tried to move, but failed. I realised that I was covered in plastic tubes. I heard a dripping noise, so I followed the sound to discover a drip bottle hanging from a pole. My nose felt uncomfortable because of some kind of peg pinching my nostrils, but I felt I was breathing better than normal.

To my surprise, there were several strange faces around my bed, together with the familiar and worried face of my granddaughter Xiaoxiao.

The strangers seemed relieved and one of them called out, 'Thank the sky, thank the earth. Respected Grandpa Zhu is still alive. Grandpa, we thought you were going to die.'

Xiaoxiao helped me to sit up and handed me a small paper cup of water. I felt thirsty, so I took a few sips. She told me I was in hospital.

'Grandpa, do you remember your talk?' Xiaoxiao asked me gently.

'My talk? What talk?'

She didn't ask again. Instead, she took a cotton bud and dipped it in water.

'Grandpa, let me wet your lips. They're dry and chapped.'

I closed my eyes and lay back down. It was all quiet in the ward. Then I heard Xiaoxiao shushing and people tiptoeing away.

I didn't open my eyes. I didn't want to – I didn't want to talk to anyone. I wanted to work out what had happened.

When I arrived at the venue, the hall was already full. I was slightly shocked by the size of the place. I had been informed that the talk would take place in a new lecture hall at the University of … I wasn't sure whether they had told me the name of the university. I didn't normally pay much attention to the premises. I didn't care where I was, and I didn't need to know – I would be transported to and from venues. I just gave talks – I carried them around in my belly.

The hall was a bit too cold for me, nothing like summer. I remembered they'd told me the air-conditioning would be controlled at an 'ethical temperature'. I had no idea what that meant, but I felt the urge to tell someone that I wanted and needed that ethical temperature; unfortunately, I didn't have a chance. Their time-management skills were superior – as soon as I was led to the lectern, someone loudly announced that the talk was commencing. They kept their promise, so I didn't waste any time waiting.

The talk was as successful and inspiring as usual – realising it might be my last talk, I got carried away. Although I was still badly out of tune after many years' practice, I offered to sing. The whole audience roared when I started to sing *Learn from Our Good Role Model Lei Feng:*

Learn from Lei Feng, our good role model
Loyal to the Red Revolution, loyal to the Party
Love or hatred, he knows where he stands
He remembers his roots
He battles for his beliefs, fights for his faith
Battles for beliefs, fights for faith
Beliefs, faith ...

Then I woke up in the hospital.

Hearing the song in my head, I opened my eyes. Xiaoxiao handed me a newspaper. I saw my picture on the front page – I had made the headlines:

Elderly Comrade Zhu Gives Excellent Talk on Lei Feng

The report was actually sincerely written:

It was poignant and moving to witness elderly Comrade Zhu Ansheng's possibly last talk on Lei Feng.

Although Zhu has never announced it officially, there is evidence that the poor state of his health might not permit him to give talks any longer. There is also a rumour that he is suffering from dementia.

Since Lei Feng's arguably heroic death, as Lei Feng's closest friend and the last person to see him alive, Zhu has devoted his time and energy to spreading Lei Feng's spirit by telling authentic first-hand stories about Lei Feng, sometimes with some of his former brotherly comrades. Needless to say, how upsetting it is to see the old generation of Chairman Mao's revolutionary soldiers passing from us one by one, leaving Zhu on his own. But he is never alone, for the sparks of the revolution have grown into a blazing fire of glory and we are all standing by.

What is Lei Feng's spirit? It is so profound that it is worth exploring all our lives.

Today we witnessed Zhu talk and sing with all his strength and we were almost prepared to see him collapse and die at the lectern, as he once indicated that he would spread Lei Feng's spirit until his last breath. He regarded it as the best way to pay his respects to his dearest comrade Lei Feng. Is it not touching?

The Martyr's Hymn

A reliable inside source has said Zhu is recovering from his heart attack but there is no information on the severity of his condition.
At this stage Zhu and his family are unavailable for comment.

If they ever asked me for comment, I would tell them I still had a living comrade.

Xiaoxiao took the newspaper and started cutting the article out.

'Grandpa, they didn't forget to bring the Lei Feng Box.'

'Good.'

'Do you want to check if everything's still there?'

Yes, I wanted to. I opened the box and took out the envelope. I wasn't really checking the photos – I wanted to look at them.

I could spot Lei Feng easily – he hadn't changed in the last fifty years, but I found it difficult to believe that the happy and good-looking young man next to him was me.

JOHN O'DONNELL

The Only Life You Could Save

Synopsis
*Summer 2004. **Michael** and **Marie**, are on their honeymoon in Ireland when Marie disappears. Police enquiries come to nothing. So Michael sets out to find Marie on his own.*

*Meanwhile, Michael's friend **Gillen** discovers Marie has met someone else.*

He decides to fly out from London to Ireland and tell his friend the bad news.

*Now on the Aran Island of Inishmore, Michael also discovers that Marie has met someone else: **Chris.** They have gone to Lough Derg together, a place of pilgrimage.*

Michael and Gillen meet up and head for Lough Derg. Michael finds Marie. But Chris, the feared rival, turns out to be a woman. There is, however, a formidable rival – Marie has turned to God.

She intends to embrace the spiritual life and join a holy order.

Gillen, having withdrawn for Michael and Marie's reunion, finds himself in a Loyalist bar. A word in support of the IRA ceasefire (we are now in 2005), and violence erupts. Gillen escapes, but only just.

Back at Lough Derg, all three set out on the drive that will take Marie back to Inishmore, when they run into the Loyalist hard men from the bar. Who take them hostage. Contriving a crime that will cast blame on the IRA and show their ceasefire to be meaningless.

But in the face of Marie's courage – born of her faith – their plan fails.

2008. Marie is now a professed nun, on her way to take up a teaching post at a school in the Central African Republic.

We go back to Michael. He draws level with Marie in time. A photographic job will take him to Barcelona tomorrow. Michael does not know a new life awaits him – but we do. Michael will find a new love, a new life, and he, too, will follow his calling.

PART ONE
1
September 2004

Oh, please ... Michael took his foot off the trembling bar rail and set his drink back down, untouched.

It wasn't the sea beyond the windows that was worrying him – a distant sea, flattened by the blessing of perspective – it was the sea beneath his feet. Way beneath. Where the thud of waves sent a great shudder through the hull and hold, the lower decks, and now, albeit fainter, up through the floor of the passenger lounge to set off that sinister chink-chinking of glasses on the bar's back shelf.

The other passengers, ranged right and left of him at the bar, didn't seem to notice. Or chose not to. But rougher – as his drink slid an inch from his fingers – it was definitely getting rougher. If it went on like this ...

Now then. Go. Do it now.

He knocked back his brandy, his third, in one, picked up the rucksack at his feet, and made his way out of the place. Past the gift shop, the Bureau de Change, the crossfire from the dark arcade of video games. Back to the main staircase. Crowded an hour ago when he'd joined the stop-start, shuffling ascent, but no one to be seen now as he dropped four flights to level D, and went left. Into a long corridor of closed cabin doors; from somewhere, a muffled voice, a man's, rising in anger: 'Says who? ... Says who?' He glanced back even as he hurried on. Down another flight of stairs at the corridor's far end – service stairs, raked at an angle best tackled backwards – and right this time. Into narrow passageway, low-lit, off limits. A shut door facing him down at the dead end. DANGER: in bold red letters. STRICTLY NO ADMITTANCE DURING VOYAGE. A hum, a low drone, leaking from the seal, and the air heavy with the smell of hot metal.

He paused now: a steadying hand on the wall as he swayed before the door. An old fear, fear of the sea, trying to turn him, but a new fear – an altogether darker fear – driving him on, and he took hold of the trembling metal handle with both hands ... and heaved. For a moment, nothing. Then a creak, a groan, and the door gave way. Set free so full-blooded a blast of sound it seemed, for a second, to assume physical form. Some poor beast or creature that fled the thundering hull, the relentless hammering of engines, and from somewhere in there – the great cave of the half-dark hold – a loose strut or stay beating out a mad beleaguered Morse.

He stepped through, sealed the door behind him, and went. Into spent air. Bad light. Moving through the cars, the tightly parked cars, parked nose to tail, soaking up the vibrations with a visible quiver of wings.

He made his way to the bow. Unslung the rucksack from his shoulder, and began. Left to right at first, then dead ahead. Straight down the line of cars. The next, the next, and the next. Pausing at each one just long enough to lift the wiper blade from the windscreen, let it fall, and hold two things in place. His last hope, and – in a word – the reason for his new fear.

MISSING.

It was, in the end, all he needed to say.

The single stark word set in black capitals above the picture of Marie. All he could say, in repeating disbelief. Missing. Save the details. The two lines of text under her smile: full name, last sighting, age (a birthday, her twenty-eighth, just days ago), colour of hair and eyes. The rest a guess, a painful lapse into the bland language of medium … average. For he no more knew her exact height and weight than he knew her shoe size; and he thought this a bad thing, a derelict thing, the night he made this simple poster, when he left the screen to stand before her wardrobe and search the sole of one of her shoes – a rainbow-coloured trainer. Still bearing a trace, grains of sand, from Patmos.

Ah … that far deserted beach. All to themselves.

Merely wistful at first, the moment, the memory. Till the aching pathos of her things – boxed, bagged, folded, on hangers, shelves – broke over him, full flood. Missing? How could she be missing when her presence resided so vividly here? In the specially chosen, the cherished and kept, this favourite … that scarf; and he knew then – with the breath of her summer dresses released to the cold night air – knew how hard it would be to let go of her possessions.

Her rainbow-coloured trainer (… size 38) still in his hand when he went back to the screen to save, and print.

He was beginning to sicken now: of heat, fumes, the heaving sea, as he braced between cars to ride out the surge and swell of one more wave, waited for the deck to come level, then carried on. Working fast. Bow to stern, back. Under the queasy spill of the safety lights, caged and shaking, high up on the hold's steel walls. A hundred cars, more. Motorbikes. Some half-dozen trucks. Twenty minutes and it was done.

He turned at the end of the last row and looked. She was everywhere. Marie.

His wife, Marie.

Smiling, secure, held tight – save for there. The cars at the front of the starboard row, where the wind, tearing over the Irish Sea, slipped through a fissure in the bow doors, to grab, lift, billow, and, but for the wiper blades, carry her far away.

He had missed just one; he made his way towards it now. His old Volvo: road-scarred, succumbing to rust. Its best years long since run. He lifted the boot lid, about to stash his bag and steal away, when: 'Hey!'

He froze. Had he heard something? A voice? A shout over the clamour? 'Hey you!'

He spun and looked up. On the gantry above him two men in boiler suits, laughing. Now a third, in the livery of the shipping line: officer's uniform, a hat. Unsmiling.

'Yes you. What the *hell* do you think you're doing?'

2

Detective Inspector John Carty pulled out a chair and sat.

He did not feel good about this. The abject figure before him, the pile of home-made posters (they'd found another batch, a box full, when they searched his car). Not good either about the assurances he had made some three weeks back. 'Leave it to us now Michael, go home'; or his promised 'close liaison' with the Met, which, in the absence of a lead, a sighting, a glimmer, had become, at best, perfunctory. And he had said as much himself, only two days, ago at a review of the still clueless case, 'perfunctory', as he closed the slender, buff-coloured folder and set it aside. The one that contained Michael's statement, names and notes. Little else. A date on the cover in urgent black italics that had only served to chasten him: *28 August 2004.*

The day of Marie's disappearance.

'We're doing everything we can,' he said now, hands clasped before him and leaning halfway over the table. 'Making every effort. Things take time Michael.'

'Yes ... I'm sure.'

'Time and more time. A pile of man hours. You wouldn't know the half of it.'

'No. I wouldn't.'

'No ... No is right ... and even then ...'

Michael looked up as the door opened. A garda came in with two cups of coffee on a tray. The older one of the two garda who were waiting when the First Officer escorted him from the ferry. The one who'd made some dumb crack about walking the plank, while the other, the younger, demanded an explanation. But beyond a shrug, a mumbled 'self explanatory', he, the reckless fool up to no good on the car deck, who 'technically' had assaulted the First Officer in a tussle over his rucksack, had failed to give one. So they called it in. A radio exchange with the station. While Michael, standing by an old contact mine, fished from the sea, splashed neutral white, and on show in the lee of the harbour wall where they'd told him to, *'Wait'*, heard:

'Oh? Right … Is that so?… Right … right you are then.'

He watched them pace from ear-shot then, and confer. Some revelation or disclosure, he imagined, borne out by their change of tone, when, a few minutes later, they walked back over. Sympathetic now. Gravely so. As the younger one opened the door of the patrol car, while the other, hovering with hands-off assistance, helped him into the back seat. Michael guessed where they were going: Blackrock Garda Station on the Ringmahon Road.

He remembered it well. Only too well.

'Every effort,' Carty said again now as the coffee was set down on the table between them. 'Rest assured.'

'Me too.'

'How's that?'

'Me too Inspector Carty, every effort. Hoping. Waiting. Trying to be patient: trying to be strong. Do you know how much effort that takes?'

'Now, Michael. I'm only saying have you the facts considered?'

'Such as?'

'Sure it's only been two weeks.'

'No. Sorry. That's not right.'

'How?'

'Two weeks, three days' – Michael looked at his watch – 'fourteen and a bit hours.'

'Aye, well, even so …'

'Sorry?'

'Not long.'

'Not long?'

'In a case the like of this, Michael, not long – in my experience.'

'Well it's a long time in mine.'

'Ach – '

'It's a goddam age.'

'And what? You think wallpapering the west of Ireland with your poster will help?'

'Hardly wallpaper.'

'Was that the plan? Giving out your number to every passer-by, to every man-jack from here to the Glenties. You think that will help?'

'It might.'

'How?'

'Let's leave it at that.'
'At what?'
'It might.'
'Ha! Divil-a-bit it will.'
'In the absence of a *better* idea then.'

Carty flinched but pressed on. 'You'll only be plagued, man. Plagued by cranks, scuts with nothing better to do. Eejits. All sorts. You'll only encourage them. Never mind disrupting our inquiries ... getting under our feet. Did you think of that?'

''Fraid not. No.'

'I dare say you didn't, no. And there'd have been ramifications, oh aye. Dead ends. Blind alleys. Wild goose chases. But how would you know till you'd followed them up? A waste of time. A complete waste of valuable police time, and resources, aye. Thin as they are.'

Carty's words snapped like kindling and Michael feared that whatever there had been between them – a liking, residual sympathy, or deeper, some unspoken solidarity of loss – was gone.

He sat back. Suddenly aware of heat; the confines of the room.

A room steeped in more grief and human confusion than one man could faithfully imagine, or bear to. For all surfaces here, walls and floor, the desk, even the sills, seemed to carry an accretion of grief, the air both dead and charged, oppressive with the imprint of all those who had sat hunched in this chair before him. But he felt their story would be different to his. Their grief visible while his was hidden: the grief of a dark street, say, a departing train, or a shadow, half-glimpsed, turning the far corner and gone irretrievably from view.

He looked up at the window and waited for the images to fade against the pale blue of the late summer sky.

'So,' he said, at length. 'You going to nick me?'

'For God's sake man. Nick you? For what?'

'Intending to wallpaper.'

Carty laughed, but immediately felt that laughter had no place here. That it was flippant, glib, or worse, suggested a lack of gravitas on his part, so when he spoke again, some measured moments later, he was serious. Sharp and hard.

'No,' he said, 'there will be no ... nicking. But I am putting you on the next boat back.'

'Inspector Carty, please don't – '

'That's it now. For the best. You've no business here.'

'No business?'

'None Michael.'

'Jesus. If only that were true.'

'Come again?'

'I said,' his anger rising now, the scarcely contained rage of these past days and nights threatening to break, and he had to bear down on himself to find the last shred of steel. 'I said, if-only-that-were-true.'

'And how's it not?'

'Oh, please. Marie's here. *Here* – for God's sake.'

'In Cork?'

'In Ireland.'

'If she is Michael – '

'If?'

'If she is, then we will find her.'

Michael watched as Carty got up from the table. The interview over, gone cold as the coffee, and concluded with that feeble caveat, but caveat enough to uncouple his desperation from their weakening resolve. (For he sensed their weakening resolve.) And wasn't there a waver, barely detectable, running under Carty's parting shot, and the way he looked at him – daggers, damn near – and the way he paused and patted him on the shoulder as he passed by: *pat-pat*. A sly, coded blow, to remind him who had the clout round here. The say-so. Might as well have patted him on the fucking head.

There there. Good boy. Nice try ...

And all at once he hated the bastard. The cuff links. Slicked back hair. Bulbous lower lip, flecked with bits of spittle. Hate. Sudden as flight ... *If? ... If? ...* And his blood began to surge and race, and he had to force himself to stop now. To stop and steady, draw breath and think, and admit to this terrible new tendency to run away with himself. Every effort, the man had said, and he had to have faith. Every effort. Yes. He had to believe.

The door opened and the same garda stepped back into the room and began to gather up the cups.

'Sure you let them go cold. Will you take another? ... No bother.'

'No thanks.'

'Tea?'

'I'm okay. Mind if I smoke?'

'Ah, no. We've the ban now, since March. No smoking. No smoking all over. The place of work as well as the pubs, the bars. The whole shebang. And weren't they after saying it wouldn't take? No chance. But there it is: the law's the law – '

'Sure is.'

' – and all the smokers out in the cold.'

'Sorry. Didn't think, that's all.'

'Aye well,' he said, quietly, looking past him, 'I'd say you have enough to think about.'

Michael heard it, a kindness, however oblique, and it touched him, deeply, his grief rose to meet it so he had to rise higher. Intent on the strength of his reply.

'Yes,' he said. 'I guess I have.'

'Be England next, with the smoking. You'll see. Well, we have you all booked up and sorted out anyways.'

'Sorry?'

'The ferry.'

'Oh ... right.'

'Away on the next.'

'Tonight?'

'19:30 she sails.'

'You mean *tonight?*'

'That's it now. You'll be into Swansea with the early birds.'

Michael looked off, beaten. Beyond the window the pale blue sky was giving way to clouds, weighty and grey. A stillness fell.

Always this: rain in the air, rain in the offing.

He watched a lone gull pass over the far harbour. He would follow it soon enough then, by night, over the dark leagues of the Irish Sea. A prospect about as welcome as the song, a song from the past – taunting, unbidden – but running, once again, through his head.

'And you may ask yourself, well, how did I get here? ... And you may ask yourself ... where is my beautiful wife?'

*

HIGHLY COMMENDED

SOPHIE O'MAHONY

Third Space

Synopsis
Jenny Gallagher, 30, suffers a nervous breakdown after the sudden death of her mother and the breakdown of an abusive relationship and subsequent suicide of her ex-boyfriend. She goes to St Ives in the hope of reconnecting with her father who walked out on the family when she was a child. While in St Ives she forms a connection with the local residents who share with her their stories of the challenges and difficulties that they have faced in life. Jenny's wayward brother Jason invites himself to stay with her in St Ives, disrupting her peace of mind and potentially her recovery. The two of them attempt to reconcile their differences and overcome their anger towards one another, particularly Jason's resentment at Jenny seemingly having abandoned her family by escaping their deprived upbringing and becoming a lawyer. At the end of the stay in St Ives Jenny meets the man she believes to be her father; however, when she has the opportunity to reveal her identity to him, she chooses not to do so as she realises that she does not need him anymore.

THIRD SPACE
Chapter 1
You know she's a girl, right?

She doesn't – didn't. She changes tense in her head because now she does. She sits on the edge of a chair, phone held to her left ear, one leg crossed firmly over the other. The buttons of her jeans dig into her stomach. She should have peed before she called.

No, I didn't know that.

She hears down the line the tapping of a pen against teeth. *Clack clack clack.* He's sizing her up, she thinks, wondering if she's worth telling the story to. For the sake of her bladder she hopes he doesn't.

He does. He did.

She's a fully fledged female, he says. A princess, no less. Irish.

Who isn't Irish? she says. She's Irish, somewhere deep inside. Way back when. If you cut her veins she would bleed [insert Irish phenomenon here, such as Guinness, shamrocks or pixie dust].

She was carried across the Irish Sea on a leaf, he explains, beginning to settle into the story.

Must have been a big leaf, she says.

It was normal-sized, he says, but when it touched the water it grew. She was meant to get a boat to Cornwall with her brothers but they left without her.

She's not surprised. Brothers, she thinks. Brothers plural – stuff of nightmares. One's bad enough. There's that phrase that is used to express exasperation: *Oh, brother.*

She really needs to pee.

Don't worry, he chuckles, she beat 'em. Turns out the leaf was faster than the boat. He makes some joke about commuting to work on foliage and arriving at the office on time. She makes herself laugh, which is difficult these days. The laughter hurts. Her bladder wails at her. She can feel her ear begin to burn. She thinks about the cells of her brain cooking under the heat of the phone. By the time the call ends a bouquet of tumours will have blossomed under her skull.

St Ia's Church, he says. You must visit. It's only up the hill from the cottage.

So where did the word 'Ives' come from? she asks as she heads to the bathroom. If she stuffs enough loo roll into the toilet bowl he won't hear her pee.

You know, I'm not sure, he says. I think it has something to do with her being a virgin.

Sure, she says, gently closing the door behind her. Saints and their sex lives.

'St Ia the Virgin'. Know what I mean? he says. Like, 'Bloody' comes from 'Our Beloved Lady'. Know what I'm talking about?

Sure, she says. Bastardisation of the English language. Laziness of the tongue. 'Blowjob' used to be 'Below Job'. She can't remember where she learned that from. She lifts up the lid of the loo and swears out loud, finding the bowl filled to the brim with shit.

Everything alright? he asks.

Yes, she says. I just remembered, I forgot to buy milk.

Ah, he says.

After this call she will phone her brother, her fucking brother (singular, thank God), who will ignore her, and then she will text him, and he will ignore that as well.

Are you sure you want the place for three months? he asks.

That is what she requested in the online booking form. That is why he asked her to call him, to check that she isn't mad or typed in the wrong dates. Three months in St Ives is a long time.

Yes, she says, three months.

There's not much to do down here, he says. Not to say that you shouldn't visit the place. He pauses. She thinks about brain cancer, her blocked toilet and the fact that she still hasn't peed. Her mother once told her a story about a relative whose name she couldn't remember that neither of them had ever met who didn't urinate for eight hours for a reason that was never explained, whose kidneys exploded from the pressure of pent-up toxins. You'll run out of things to do pretty quickly, he says eventually. Not that I want to ruin a sale. We're famous for our cuisine.

Three months, she says, putting her hand under her groin and applying pressure. Please.

And it'll just be you, or –

He doesn't need to know. As long as she pays him what he's owed and doesn't smoke inside the cottage and double locks the front door and remembers to take the rubbish and recycling out on Wednesdays he doesn't need to know if it'll be just her, or –

I'll be with a friend, she says.

Grand, he says. You know, if you and your *friend* are looking for something to do, there's a hotel up the road which does a great spa deal –

She does not want a kidney transplant (or brain cancer, or a blocked toilet). She unzips her jeans, pulls down her pants, sits on the edge of the bath and pisses right into the tub. The relief is intense. She lets out a soft moan.

You alright? he says.

Yes, she says. Found some milk.

Chapter 2

Her grandmother's name is Niamh. Her mother's name is Sabhbh. Niamh means *bright* or *radiant*. Sabhbh means s*weet and lovely.*

Her name is Jenny. It means

Cornish: far and yielding

Celtic: white wave

Animal husbandry: a female donkey or ass

Her name is Jennifer Gallagher. Only certain people say her full name, like the doctor or teachers at school when going through the morning register. When her name is said in full she feels sick and the floor moves up and down like she's on a boat going over waves. It means she is in trouble or about to be given terrible news. So when she's asked for her name she gives it as Jenny and if she asked if it's short for anything she says No, my name's Jenny, just Jenny.

Well, Just Jenny, says the taxi driver. You look in a bit of a state, that's for sure.

But for sure. It would have been a three minute walk from the station to Keepsake Cottage. The walk would have taken her down a secluded alleyway – not the kind you get in London with the muggers and the murderers and the rapists and the overpowering odour of piss and shit, the kind surrounded by trees and rockeries and a view of the sea to the right as you come down the slope, the smell of salt hanging heavy in the air. She would have turned left at the end of the alleyway, past a fish and chip shop with a crowd of gulls hovering outside, up a tiny road that didn't seem big enough for her to fit through let alone a car, and there just ahead of her next to a shop selling crystals and offering to tell your fortune: a tiny house offering two bedrooms, two bathrooms, a downstairs loo, a living room, a dining room, and a fully functioning kitchen. THREE MINUTE WALK TO THE STATION, FIVE MINUTE WALK TO THE BEACH, said the rental website, perfectly accurate in its assessment of time and distance as Jenny would have discovered for herself had she not halfway through the seven hour train journey from London to St Ives come down with a terrible, probably incurable virus which left her barely able to get out of her train seat to chuck up a semi-digested BLT out of the window onto the Devonshire countryside, so that was why the taxi was doing for her what otherwise would have been a three minute walk. Stops you from getting wet I suppose, the taxi driver had said as he loaded her luggage (one medium-sized suitcase) into the boot of the car. She hadn't even noticed it was raining.

You alright, Just Jenny? says the taxi driver. Did you hear what I just said?

No, says Jenny. Normally her response to a question like that would be: No, sorry, would you mind repeating that? or Goodness, I was completely away with the fairies there, wasn't I? or Yes, I heard you, the answer is 1935, the year that Mussolini invaded Abyssinia (now Ethiopia). But she has no voice left and her throat is so dry that it hurts to swallow.

I said, says the taxi driver, is there anyone that you can call?

There's no one that she can call. Everyone is either dead, dead to her or she is dead to them. If the taxi driver held a gun to her head right now and made her ring someone on the condition that they picked up he'd have no choice but to blow her brains out. She used to watch Who Wants To Be A Millionaire on the telly when she was younger. She would hide behind a cushion whenever a contestant exercised their right to Phone A Friend, just in case the friend was not around or they'd had a falling out the night before and the friend decided that they still weren't speaking to them. Of course, such a thing was never left to chance, she was aware of this, she knew that the friend would be sitting backstage somewhere with a cup of tea in one hand and a biscuit in the other, being looked after by an enthusiastic intern with a clipboard and a headset, but she always wondered why the friend let the phone ring for as long as they did before picking up (even now the sound of pipsset her teeth on edge). She would never do that to a friend, not in a gazillion years, not that any friend of hers would go on Who Wants To Be A Millionaire. Not that she has any friends right now.

 Her mother once told her a story about a friend's cousin (she couldn't remember which friend it was, it frustrated her no end) who one day got on a train from Edinburgh to Birmingham and found herself sitting opposite a man dressed in a very smart suit. Mr Smart Suit was reading a newspaper, the Financial Times no less, while the friend's cousin made do with a magazine that she had picked up from WHSmith. There was an article in the magazine about, swear to God, this complete *miracle* of a face cream that removed all lines and wrinkles after three months' use (there were Before and After photos to prove it) and Mr Smart Suit was quietly reading his own articles, probably about the Market and Money and Shares (yawn), and so that was all fine. But about half an hour into the journey Mr Smart Suit suddenly put down his newspaper and just *stared* at the friend's cousin, and not in a lovey-dovey, wide-eyed kind of way, not even in an annoyed way (she had a habit of humming whatever tune popped into her head), but he just kept looking at her and wouldn't turn away. This went on for a very long time. The friend's cousin thought about saying something to Mr Smart Suit, something along the lines of: Didn't your mother ever tell you it was rude to stare? Or: If you want my number you only have to ask (she must have been quite confident, this friend's cousin). Shortly after thinking all these thoughts she noticed another man, also in a suit, but with a coffee stain down the front of it and a large, unkempt bald patch on the top of his head, sitting across the aisle and staring at Mr Smart Suit in just the same way as Mr Smart Suit was staring at her. For one hysterical moment the friend's cousin thought that maybe there was a staring contest or something going on in her carriage, not that anyone had told her about it, but then Mr Bald Patch had suddenly stood up and hovered over her and said in the calmest voice she had ever heard: Madam, I advise that you leave this carriage *now*. She felt a chill run all the way down her spine when he said that and left the carriage pretty damn quickly with legs that felt like jelly. The train stopped for a while at Doncaster which annoyed all the passengers. Some tweeted about it. Then a number of police and paramedics got on and the friend's cousin saw through the window Mr Bald Patch talking to one of the officers who was making notes in a pocketbook. As it turned out, Mr Bald Patch was a doctor and Mr Smart Suit had been staring at the friend's cousin not because she'd blow dried her hair into luscious curls that morning or because she was humming *Lovin' You* too loudly, but rather because he was stone-cold *dead*. And when her mother told her this story Jenny said how awful it must have been for his friends and family to have to go and collect their deceased loved one from a train, and her mother said that it wouldn't be the most awful thing to happen to anyone, no, the most awful thing would be if no one came forward to claim him.

Just Jenny? says the taxi driver. Who you gonna call then?

My mum, Jenny croaks.

That'll make you feel better, I'm sure, the taxi driver says, smiling at her in the rearview mirror.

They arrive at Keepsake Cottage. He takes her suitcase out of the boot of the car, locates the key under the flower pot as per the emailed instructions, unlocks the door and guides her upstairs to one of the bedrooms. He removes her socks and shoes as she collapses onto the bed. As darkness falls on her she wonders if he might violate her, which she thinks she would be fine with as long as he doesn't wake her, but no, he is that rare breed of person, a decent human being who gets her a glass of water and leaves it on the bedside cabinet next to her and the last thing Just Jenny sees before she blacks out is him slipping a small piece of paper under the glass and the terrified face of a man as he falls to the ground faster than he could have ever imagined.

HIGHLY COMMENDED

SARAH REYNOLDS

The Haven

Synopsis
On 20th September 1995, fifteen-year-old Emma Granger sent a bunch of flowers to her parents then disappeared.

Twenty years later, Emma's best friend, Kate is at home with a new baby and feeling deranged with sleep-deprivation. Emma's mother, Sybil, is suffering from dementia and has become convinced that a TV presenter on Welsh-language television is in fact, her long-lost daughter. Each woman has her own secrets and her own, painful reasons for wanting to find Emma after all this time.

When a body is unearthed in Roedale Park, it is not the end of their search, but the beginning. Interwoven with the pursuit for Emma, are the events of twenty years before. By the end of the novel, the past catches up with the present and we understand at last how 'Emma' died and how 'Alys' was born.

THE HAVEN
Earlsdon Park Nursing Home, Surrey, 2015.
It was almost midday and the flowers still hadn't come. Sybil felt giddy at the possibility that they might not come at all. She stood by the window with her arms by her sides, hands balled into fists. The stiff strips of the vertical blinds quivered under her breath.

'Daft tart!' she said out loud.

It was the impetus she needed to tweak the blinds apart and peer outside. The porch was empty. She let out a jubilant snort and cast her eyes over the forecourt. Earlsdon Park was just so, its prim lawns and trimmed hedges orderly in all weathers. The only movement came from a stand of ash trees at the far end of the residents' front garden. Sybil watched their fluffy heads sway on invisible autumn currents, mesmerisingly slow, as if they were underwater.

It was a grand old place, Earlsdon Park, a Georgian mansion – listed to boot! Clive was a great admirer of Georgian architecture. Its boxy symmetry and buttoned up propriety appealed to his puritanical streak.

The Haven

When he'd first found the place on SuperiorResidentialServices.co.uk, he'd gushed over its features: a sweeping driveway and grand old staircase, not to mention the five mile golf-course draped over its surrounding acres. He'd declared the place perfect – the best home that money could buy. The second best, Sybil had thought, privately, the first best being already occupied by Clive himself, his new wife and his new daughter. Still, Sybil didn't mind too much. She liked to think that his becoming a father again at the age of fifty-eight was punishment enough. How old was the child by now? Nine? Ten? Sally or Sammy or something. Come to think of it, wasn't Sammy the name of Clive's childhood dog? It wouldn't be beyond Clive to name his child after a dog.

Sybil's eyes raked the driveway in search of intruders brandishing flowers. Not a soul. With her fingertip on the glass, she followed the unwavering line of the driveway towards the home. Here, the path widened to embrace a greying fountain that had been disconnected in anticipation of frost. She missed its steady sibilance in the winter months. If she stood in the exact centre of the central pane of her window, Sybil could align her nose with the valve and make her reflection appear to be taking a drink from the fountain. This was pleasing. She had her very own 'water feature'. Daytime television was always on about water features.

At that moment, Janice clattered in with a flapping clipboard and a breezy smile.

'Hello Sybil, it's time for your pills!'

Underneath her white plastic pinny, she wore a smart navy uniform with brass buttons that made Sybil think of a bellboy. She wanted to ask her why she cut her hair so short and wore no makeup. She had fine cheekbones and pretty hazel eyes. Why must she cultivate this charade of masculinity? If Sybil were her mother she would ask her bluntly, 'Don't you like being a woman?'

Sybil smiled politely and swallowed her pills. She was not Janice's mother; she was nobody's mother anymore.

'Now then Janice, I shouldn't like to create a fuss but I do hope that new coloured girl knows I don't accept flowers.'

'Her name is Nora and we don't use that word anymore, Sybil. It's racist.'

'Racist?'

Sybil felt rather perturbed. She didn't consider herself a racist but she was clearly no longer 'au fait' with the correct terminology. Wasn't it rather crude to refer to someone as black? Coloured sounded, to her, a much more pleasant word.

'Are you coming down for afternoon tea, Sybil? The entertainment's due at half two.'

131

'Perhaps later.'

Just as Janice reached the door, her hand poised on the sloping handle, Sybil called out to her.

'Nothing's come for me, has it Janice?'

'No flowers, Sybil, no.'

'She's cruel you know –'

'Come on now, don't distress yourself. Why don't we see what's on the telly? What is it now… two o'clock? 'Loose Women' has finished but you like 'Doctors' don't you?'

Television was Janice's preferred choice of anaesthetic for her clients.

By the time she'd closed the door, Sybil was sitting in the easy chair, a rug over her knees, the remote control perched on the armrest. Emma's Australian stories would be on soon. *No matter where you are, you're my guiding star.* She could see her now, sitting on the sofa at home with her Findus Crispy Pancakes. *Neighbours* first, then *Home and Away* and a nice fat slice of Viennetta. Watching Emma's programmes made Sybil feel closer to her somehow. One day, when they met again – for she was certain they would – at least they'd have something to talk about.

A drama was unfolding on the screen before her; a doctor paying a house call, a woman collapsed behind her own front door. Sybil stared at the flashing colours on the screen until her eyes lost focus.

On this very day, twenty years ago, Sybil had received a knock on the door. At first she'd ignored it. She'd been in the bath for one thing and for another, her right foot had been incapacitated at the time, Maddox Graham's mouth clamped around her big toe like an anemone. He'd made her squeal with that mouth. There'd been the David Mellor / Antonia de Sancha scandal a year or so before and now everyone was into toe sucking. It simply had to be tried! Clive had always teased Sybil that she had the feet of a peasant. When she'd mentioned this to Maddox he'd bitten her instep and told her that he had barbarous tastes.

The visitor had gone for the bell next, a long, painful trill. Prising her toe from Maddox's lips, Sybil had risen out of the bath, feeling like Venus herself. The dressing gown was new, a gift from Maddox, from New York. He'd had her initials embroidered onto the pocket. How strange she thought, to buy one's lover a gift, and have it embroidered with the surname of another man.

She galloped down the stairs, leaving a trail of dark footprints on the carpet. The moment she opened the door, an angry gust of autumn air rushed inside. A dollop of bubbles slid from her shin, landing on the hall rug like meringue. The bell presser had given up and gone. Standing in his place – for it was later confirmed that Wendy Paton's boy had made the delivery – was a small rattan basket with a tall loop handle, the type that a bridesmaid might tote down the aisle. It was neatly packed with orange gerberas, fire lilies, yellow roses and lisianthus. Too small to be from Maddox. Too thoughtful to be from Clive. As Sybil scooped up the basket, the wind slammed the front door closed.

'Maddox?'

She heard his heavy footsteps above her, the sound of bathwater gargling away. Seized by curious delight, she tugged at the small envelope stapled to the cellophane. Her own name and address were written there in biro, an unfamiliar hand – later confirmed to be that of the florist, Wendy Paton. Inside, a standard white card, blank as a winter's sky. Sybil often wondered what had become of that card. Had it been taken into evidence? Destroyed, perhaps by Clive? She would like to have kept it.

Laughter jangled down the corridor. Janice enjoyed a joke with the residents.

'Come on Ken, we'll have you dancing yet!'

Ken slept in the room next to Sybil's. She heard him shambling down the corridor with his walker, huffing as he passed her door. Any moment, Janice would poke her head around and ask if Sybil was coming for a 'good old-fashioned sing along.'

Sybil feigned sleep and rolled the pad of her fingertip over the seed pearls sewn onto her cardigan. It was a cream cashmere cardigan that did not belong to her but to which she had taken a shine ever since it had been wrongly delivered to her chest of drawers several days ago. She counted seven seed pearls. Seven tiny planets orbiting a brilliant sequin. Eleven similar galaxies clustered across her shoulders. She'd counted them. Eleven planets times seven stars is seventy-seven. Seven years more than her current age. Seven more years to endure. Wasn't it written in the stars?

When she opened her eyes, the television had been turned off and the light was drawing dim. The blinds cast dark bars across the back wall. It must be teatime soon. A little thrill shot through her from chin to shin; there'd been no sign of flowers.

There were footsteps in the hallway. The door crashed open and in swung Hillary, wearing a nightie and clutching a doll.

'Did I leave my good slippers in here, duck?'

Before Sybil could respond, Hillary was scrabbling under the bed like a kitten.

'Things go missing in this place…'

Sybil didn't deign to respond. Instead, she pressed her buzzer. The light came on but there was no sign of Janice. Hillary was ferreting under the dresser by now, yanking out wodges of private correspondence from between the skirting board and the walnut sideboard. Heat spread prickly fingers around Sybil's throat. She'd grown up with that sideboard – a relic from Aunty Glad and Uncle Sid – still perfectly serviceable, rather charming really, whatever Clive said. Since Janice refused to post any more of Sybil's letters to Emma, she'd taken to posting her letters there – a place where only Emma would know to look.

Sybil pressed the buzzer again and again until finally, Janice appeared.

'This is the third time that woman has been in here! Either buy her a new pair of slippers or lock the nutcase up!'

'We have no nutcases in here Sybil.'

'The barmy army.'

Janice ushered Hillary away.

When she was alone once more, Sybil sat on the carpet by the sideboard, her letters strewn about her like flotsam. She dragged them into her arms and sobbed. Tears came easily these days, as indulgent and cleansing as a good soak in the bath. From the sleeve of her cardigan she drew out a handkerchief and pressed it to her face. Janice did not approve of handkerchiefs.

'Use a tissue, Sybil,' she'd say when she found another crusty bundle in the laundry basket, 'It's so much more hygienic.'

Sybil blew her nose noisily and blotted the tears that had gathered under her chin. She screwed up her sorrow like a fist and stuffed the handkerchief back into her sleeve. No sense in becoming maudlin. Onwards and upwards: wrapping her fingertips over the thick lip of the dresser, she hauled herself up into a standing position. She lingered there a moment, stooped over the dresser, her laboured breaths disturbing Nanny Yarden's lace doily. The longer she stared at it, the more the dainty lace picots seemed to dance before her eyes. She nudged the doily aside and ran her finger over the ghostly stain of water.

She'd wanted to catch Maddox before he got dressed, while he was still warm and wet and bubbly. With no thought for a dish or a coaster or a doily, she'd placed the flowers on the walnut sideboard and leapt up the stairs two at a time. She found Maddox in the bedroom, brazenly drying himself on a towel belonging to Clive. He was as naked as a hairy man can be. Thick black curls crawled across his chest, his back, over his buttocks. Sybil was at once repelled and enthralled. She'd only ever known Clive, the narrow spine he turned towards her each night, pale and speckled as a hen's egg.

The Haven

Maddox turned at the sound of her footsteps.

'It wasn't...?'

'Clive? No.'

'Thank God for that! I thought I was about to be challenged to a duel or something!'

'I can't imagine Clive fighting for anything... least of all me.'

'I'd fight for you baby,' he said, sliding a finger into the belt of her bathrobe and pulling her towards him. The robe fell open and he ploughed his hands inside, grabbing fistfuls of wobbly flesh, making Sybil shriek with laughter.

'So who was it?' he said, sweeping her onto the bed, 'Your other lover?'

He bit her earlobe when she didn't reply.

'It was no one!' she giggled, and he bit her harder.

'Really! It was no one!'

They spent the remainder of the afternoon between Sybil's best Egyptian cotton sheets, (thread count: 600), undoing all the good of the bath.

It was a policewoman who first noticed the flowers on the sideboard.

'Would you mind if we go through to the other room?' she said, 'Only I'm allergic to lilies.'

As Sybil led PC Blakey through to the lounge, she saw the question form in Clive's mind: *Where did they come from?*

She felt her heart flutter against her ribcage and before Clive had spoken the words out loud, she answered,

'Oh yes, the flowers. I was in the bath.'

Perhaps it was the strident note in Sybil's voice that caught PC Blakey's attention. She raised her long nose as if she had caught the scent of a lie. Sybil had no choice but to bluster on.

'The strangest thing... they were addressed to me but the card was blank...'

Clive was instantly impatient.

'Well who are they from?'

'That's the point. I don't know.'

'Well you must have some idea. One of your ladies from the Golf Club? Church?'

'It's not important, Clive. Right now, we need to focus on Emma.'

Later, as PC Blakey was about to leave, she asked to see the card that came with the flowers.

'The card? Of course. It's still –'

It was then that Sybil noticed the basket was leaking. In the yellow glow of the hallway, water collected at its base like urine.

'Clive, would you get a cloth?'

Blakey plucked the florist's card from its envelope and inspected the logo.

'Cornucopia.'

'Yes. Lovely little shop on the high street…'

Sybil's voice trailed off. Blakey's eyes levelled with her own. She spoke in a low tone.

'We could talk in private about the flowers…'

'I don't know what you're implying,' Sybil replied.

Clive returned with a hand towel and began to mop up the water.

'Don't use that,' said Sybil, 'Why didn't you get the cloth from the kitchen, like I said?'

'Stop fussing woman – it's just a bloody towel.'

'I'll take this, if I may?' said PC Blakey, holding up the florist's card as if it were a courtroom exhibit.

'Of course, if you think it might help… although I fail to see how?'

'We need to follow all possible lines of enquiry.'

'Of course.'

'You have my card. If there are any developments, or if she comes home, please call me directly. In the meantime, I promise you, we're doing everything we can.'

Clive shook the officer's hand.

'Thank you, PC Blakey,' he said, then, as an after thought. 'Don't work too hard now!'

It was this, strange parting sentence that would be held against him in the months that followed. Sybil cringed even as her husband spoke the words. He was always so very terrible with words.

Sybil felt a little better once she was sitting back in her chair with her blanket over her knees. She smoothed out its rumples and composed herself, tapping her thumbs against each fingertip: Peter Pointer, Finger Tall, Ruby Ring, Baby Small. Back and forth, ten times over until she felt right as rain.

She reached for the remote control. Emma wouldn't be on the television until six but she might catch the end of Pastor Derek. If not, then she'd just have to make do with one of the others. There was a different pastor on every channel from 580 to 590. Most of them were American and while she relished their message, she did question whether the word of God ought not to be delivered with a greater reverence for basic grammar: *Acceptance be the path to righteousness. Don't be puttin' a question mark where God done put a period.*

Pastor Derek, however, was different – he was English. He had a kind smile and a pithy turn of phrase and his accent, though Northern, was not offensively so. She'd never heard of his ministry before but she was reassured to learn that she could join its ranks without ever leaving her armchair. He told her every day, 'It's my great honour to come into your home and worship with you.'

His chivalry made her blush.

From Pastor Derek, she'd learned that rain falls on the just and the unjust alike. From Pastor Derek she'd learned that God is in control and He does *not* make mistakes. From Pastor Derek she'd learned that there is a purpose in our pain; that you can choose to be bitter, or choose to be better. You can choose to *go* through it or *grow* through it. You can be a whiner, or you can be a warrior.

Sybil's favourite part of his programme was its glorious crescendo, at which point Pastor Derek would be joined on stage by a chap on a keyboard and a lady with an African drum and they'd sing out various epithets:

'Lift up your heads and lift up your eyes, for the glory of God shall be revealed!'

'The Lord is with us and among us!'

'Ho! Raise your hands and give God praise!'

'Zappappa! Whoo!'

Sometimes Pastor Derek whooped himself hoarse and while he was taking a sip of water, his wife would step into the breach, her face a glaze of ecstasy:

'The work of the Lord is Shabbbabba satororo! Hilaba jojodona Allelulia!'

It really was quite a show. Jolly stirring stuff.

'Pray the pain away,' Pastor Derek had told her.

Sybil prayed so often that she began to think of her prayers as one, long, open-ended conversation with God. At first she'd asked Him why He had taken her children from her. This was a mistake. It was not her place to question His methods. In the fullness of time, she would bear witness to the slow unsheathing of His great plan. Pastor Derek assured her that if she submitted to His truth, wonderful things would begin to happen. Pastor Derek was right.

There were small signs at first: a white feather on her pillow, a favourite song on the wireless, a Peach Melba yoghurt instead of the usual Autumn Fruits. Then, one balmy August afternoon last year, through the power of television, the Lord Almighty saw fit to reward Sybil's obedience. He woke her from her slumbers with the booming voice of a sofa salesman: 'Yours for just two nine nine and zero percent interest!'

Fishing out the remote control from where it had worked its way down between the cushion and the chair wing, Sybil jabbed indiscriminately at the buttons in an attempt to dim the sound.

God would not be silenced.

He had a message that only Sybil could hear. Channel after channel jumped across the screen – snatches of words, music, images, none of it made sense to her until finally, miraculously, it did. God was the force in her fingertips that day; the day she summoned Channel 134 on her television set and came face to face with an angel. She was dressed in magisterial robes of gold and purple and sitting on a throne of light. An archangel hovered above her, speaking the language of heaven as he placed a silver crown upon her head. The angel looked directly at Sybil and smiled.

For now we see through a glass, darkly; but then face to face.
The face Sybil saw was Emma's.

SALLY SKINNER

The Fleeting

Synopsis
The vineyards of Burgundy, 1904. The daughter of a late, great scientist has nine months to uncover the secrets of her past, so she can face her future as a mother.

* * *

The pioneering physiologist and cinematographer ÉTIENNE-JULES MAREY spends the summers of the 1880s with his assistant DEMENŸ in his Paris laboratory, and winters with his daughter FRANCESCA and HER MOTHER in Naples. Invited to Paris for the first time, twelve-year-old Francesca enthrals her friend LEOLA with tales of her father's fascinating 'secret life'. But when Marey instructs her to call him uncle in public, she's dismayed to realise 'I am the secret'. Years later, she feels abandoned again when Leola contracts cholera and Marey, hearing rumours their friendship has become 'unnatural', denies them his help. Leola recovers but Francesca's mother dies, leaving Marey shattered. When he introduces Francesca to NOEL, a heraldic artist, she has some doubts about her suitor's motives but agrees to marry him.

This storyline is interwoven with a later period: the year following Marey's death in 1904. Francesca and Noel are living at the family vineyard, the Domaine de la Folie. *The appellation is fitting: Francesca is lost in grief, and pregnant. When an old friend lets slip a grudge against Demenÿ, she suspects the past holds one last secret. She travels to Paris and discovers Marey never received her plea for help, having been detained by a painful legal battle initiated by Demenÿ. Back in Burgundy, Francesca finds herself alone with her memories and the maddening Mistral wind, until her baby's kick wakes her up to reality. After dealing with Marey's estate, Noel returns with Leola. Ultimately, Francesca's friend proves no threat to the marriage: Noel has waited through Francesca's grief, confirmed by a new family crest that unites their past and present.*

A Shadow

A shivering shift, the train gathers speed, Vesuvius slips from sight. I have broken through, the heat and dust of Naples behind me, for it's the first day of June and I'm bound for France. On my lap lies an English novel stolen from Mamma's collection. Across its unreadable pages I have pasted French stamps, drawings of dancers torn from a ballet programme, the tail feather of a pelican: ephemera from my father's secret life.

The letter falls from its place. I smooth open the stained pages and read for the hundredth time the plans for my arrival at the Gare du Nord.

'Monsieur *De*menÿ. Monsieur Deme*n*ÿ.'

However I inflect it, the name of Papa's assistant sounds suitably exotic in the empty carriage. I close my eyes and picture the destination I've so often painted for my schoolfriends. A hive of intellectuals, artists and elegant women; a spider web of boulevards; a dizzying constellation of cafés and salons. An idea of a place. A dream.

Paris.

Leola's dark eyes would sparkle at the word. 'What does your father do there?'

'Work, of course. He's a physiologist. I'm to spend the summer with him, Mamma has agreed to it.'

'And what will *you* do?'

'Oh, a lot of work during the day. And then whatever Papa does in the evening.'

'Go to the ballet, I expect.'

I enact an elaborate curtsey; Leola laughs, flicks water up at my face. We've spent so many hours by the creek that snakes through the grounds of my parents' villa and into the Bay - whole days talking, talking, talking until I can barely distinguish her voice from mine as we trade marbles, storybooks, shells, theories. But with Naples sliding into the distance, those conversations already belong to another time, another me.

I walk into the open-sided carriage and loosen the hatpins Mamma insisted on fixing herself this morning. Amongst other dangers she has warned me against travel sickness, but the motion of the train is in perfect unison with my thoughts, taking my restlessness and spending it on the tracks. When I lean over the handrail to watch the railway lines curve into the landscape, the blast of air tears the hat from my head and a laugh from my mouth, sends my hair streaming and empties my mind of thoughts of home.

* * *

In the morning I make my way to the dining car. Passengers that must have boarded the train overnight now crowd the white tables with their coffee cups and newspapers. Few seem to notice me: a twelve-year-old girl in a corner seat, waiting for Paris to emerge beneath a brightening sky.

We move slowly through scrubby patches of farmland studded with shacks, windmills and cattle. My fellow travellers finish their drinks and begin to gather their possessions, yet the horizon offers only a clump of greyish edifices beneath tall, smoking chimneys: were it not for the bustling confidence around me, I might have thought we'd made one big circuit and arrived back in Naples. As we draw closer, the grey clump resolves into separate buildings in various shades and stages of decay. Lines of laundry flap between windows on the upper floors, while doorways form makeshift market stalls, piles of vegetables spilling onto the carts and pavements. One of the larger buildings resembles a vast, gaping mouth, topped with a huge pediment of iron and glass that reflects the rising sun. The light takes on a greenish hue as the train passes under the roof and, with a final, histrionic sneeze that makes me start, comes to a halt.

On the platform I find myself adrift in a sea of shoulders and noise. I try not to cough as the tang of hot oil, smoke and steam invades the back of my throat. After the sleepy calm of the carriage, the cacophony of shouts, hissing engines, clanging doors and shrieking whistles is like an assault, and I struggle to find my bearings whilst being swept in the general direction of the crowd. Just before my confusion gives way to panic, billows of steam dissolve before a face. Dark moustache, gentle eyes.

'Mademoiselle Francesca?'

I nod and the moustache spreads over a smile.

'Georges Demenÿ.' Accent on the ÿ. 'Enchanté.'

The skin around his eyes crinkles like my father's, although he must be much younger. He locates my case from the luggage wagon, offers his arm and escorts me through the high, echoing spaces of the station's interior, out through the stone pillars of the entrance and towards a coach.

I take a deep breath to rid myself of the platform's stench of soot and sweat, only to fill my nostrils with a potent mix of sewage and smoke, yeast and manure. I give distracted answers to Demenÿ's questions about my journey, struggling to keep pace with him as a thousand sights and sounds rush my senses. It's still early but the streets are already full of people whispering and shouting and calling to each other, the private language of my family home suddenly multiplied and estranged.

'The boulevard Delessert, driver, if you please.' Demenÿ settles into his coach seat and begins to examine a sheaf of papers, allowing me to gaze out of the window without feeling impolite. Gradually, the motley architecture surrounding the station gives way to more uniform streets, honey-coloured and tree-lined.

I've spent hours questioning my father about his summers in Paris, studying every map and guide to the city I could find. Now that I'm here, nothing in the relentless procession of shop fronts and street signs - flashes of blue and white that I strain to read as we pass - affords me any clue to our location. When the road takes on the width of a river, my curiosity bursts its banks.

'Monsieur Demenÿ, where are we?'

He lifts his head from his papers and glances out of the window. 'About to cross the Champs-Élysées.'

I move closer to the glass and try to press the composition of trees and street lamps, carriages and monuments into my memory. Formal rows of linden trees flash past, dividing the view into a magic lantern display of iconic sights.

'Not far now, Mademoiselle Francesca.'

'Please, would you call me Cece? I think I like it better.'

'It will be my pleasure,' he says. 'And you may call me Georges.'

His hands are lightly freckled. I glance at my own, see the fingernails are rimed with dirt and sit on them. 'Will we see Papa today, do you think?'

At the mention of my father something unreadable passes across his eyes, but is gone in an instant. It could have been the shadow of a lamppost. 'Professeur Marey gave me the express direction to bring you to the Station Physiologique as soon as you've unpacked. You are not too tired?'

'Not at all.'

'I have a small errand to make first.' He raps on the ceiling to halt the coach, hops down and disappears into a side street. A clock tower casts its long shadow across the square to my right; by craning my neck I can make out the time as a little after eight. Back home, Leola will be feeding her chickens. Mamma will still be asleep...

'Thank you, driver.' Demenÿ swings himself back into the coach and, in the same fluid movement, presents me with a small jar.

'Lampblack Pigment,' I read. 'Is it for painting?'

'In a manner of speaking.' He takes back the jar and pockets it with a wink.

A short time later the coach pulls up outside an imposing terrace of houses, a gently curving façade of ivory scored with thick, horizontal lines. Demenÿ alights from the coach and helps me down.

'Mademoiselle Cece, the boulevard Delessert,' he announces with a slight bow. An emerald green door opens to reveal a vestibule with polished marble floors and Demenÿ introduces me to the housekeeper, a middle-aged woman who eyes me pensively when she thinks I'm not looking.

'Elise will show you to your room,' he says. 'I'll wait for you here, say half an hour?'

It doesn't take long to unpack. I place my book of secrets on the bedside table, hang my travelling duster in the wardrobe, then position my case under the window and sit on it. The room is spacious and simply adorned with a circular wall mirror of convex glass. No clock. I fill a glass bowl from the jug of water beside it, wash my face and hands, change into a pinafore dress and leave the room.

There's a boy on the stairs. He's older than me, I think, by a couple of years. We lock eyes for a moment then he dashes through a doorway and is gone. I hear a woman whisper as I pass, but if the boy responds it's too muffled to make out.

Demenÿ is reading in an armchair by the hat stand.

'Georges.'

He looks up as I descend the last spiral of stairs. 'Ah, Mademoiselle Cece. Shall we?'

* * *

It's only a short walk to his place of work, but Demenÿ seems to grow in stature as we make our way through the Bois de Boulogne. The Station Physiologique is a large, squarish chalet with black beams and low eaves, nestled among trees in an unpromising corner of the park. My companion points out the large clearing in front of the building, marked with two concentric oval tracks.

'The outer track is for men,' he says, 'and the inner one for animals. We shall be glad of your help with all kinds of creatures – dogs, sheep, donkeys. Elephants.'

'Elephants?'

'Yes, but not today. The Ministry of War has sent us horses.'

As if to demonstrate the fact, a whinny sounds from the trees. Three dark horses are tethered in the shade and a man is examining one of their legs. It's been a matter of weeks since I last saw him but, bent at the waist, he looks stouter than I remember and at the same time, inexplicably, more frail. I feel a small, shameful stab of pity.

'Papa!'

His face creases into a broad smile. 'Francesca, here you are at last!'

'It's Cece, Papa.'

'Is it, now? And how is one supposed to keep pace with such an inconstant daughter?' His beard twitches with mock indignation.

'Mamma sends her love.'

Demenÿ, who has hung back a short distance, now takes his leave with another bow and withdraws to the chalet.

'Is she well?' my father asks.

'Quite well.' He throws me a knowing glance, then gestures to the hangar that stands behind a section of the outer track: a larger version of the shelter he built near our villa, around ten metres wide and at least as deep. We go inside, treading on the black velvet that lines the floor, sides and ceiling of the structure, my father proudly holding forth on the 'near absolute' blackness they have managed to achieve with the latest funds from the Ministry. I am sat on a velvet-covered crate and given the mysterious task of cutting small shapes out of white paper. A game to distract a child? The idea troubles me for a moment, but with Demenÿ nearby once more I cannot speak to Papa as freely as I might back home. I take up the scissors.

The lampblack, it seems, is to play a crucial part in today's experiment: Demenÿ daubs it onto the right-hand side of each horse's coat, dimming its reflective lustre, whilst little heaps of diamonds, triangles, rings, crosses and hearts accumulate in the folds of my dress.

'Professeur,' calls Demenÿ. 'The mare is settled now, I think.'

My father takes a handful of white shapes, pronounces them 'perfect' and proceeds to glue them to the side of the mare's leg joints.

'Point of hip. Stifle. Hock. Fetlock.' The other horses, a leggy colt and a heavyset Ardennes, whicker and stamp in the shade. 'Point of shoulder. Elbow. Knee. Fetlock. Alright, come with me, Cece.'

I follow him towards the camera, mounted in the centre of the field and directed towards the hangar. From here, my morning's work begins to make sense: as Demenÿ leads the dark horses across the field of view, the white shapes stand out like stars against the black background.

'Movement – any movement – is a complicated thing,' says Papa. 'With chronophotography, we can increase the shutter speed by greater and still greater degrees; produce more and more images; slow time to see more and more detail, invisible to the eye alone. But too much information and all we see is a blur.' He passes his hand so quickly before my eyes, I briefly flinch, then laugh. His face, lit up as I have never seen, assumes a sudden gravity. 'We must decide what to present, what to eliminate. Do you see?'

'Yes, Papa.'

'This way we can focus on the part of the movement that interests us. In this case, the effect of length of limb.'

I've always loved to hear my father talk about his work. Since first hearing the word, I have relished the numerous syllables of *chronophotography*, stringing them together like pearls to impress my friends, and I have managed to form a vague understanding of its powers. That it produces a set of photographs of a moving object, recording the successive phases of its motion. That my father can layer these photographs in a single frame and read the language of movement, as clearly as the curve of a graph. But seeing these powers in practice is a different matter entirely, a storybook come to life.

The rest of the day settles into an agreeable pattern: I attend to the horses, Papa the photographic equipment, while Demenÿ shuttles tirelessly between us. Back in Posillipo, I've often wondered about the aide who claims my father's presence each summer. Papa always speaks highly of his assistant and I know his connections were critical in securing the funds they needed to build the Station. Still, I have resented this rival for my father's affections. Seeing Demenÿ now, moving calmly and efficiently about the place, taking the strain off his employer whenever he can and freeing him to concentrate on his latest obsession, I chide myself. He's like an obedient shadow. The perfect préparateur.

* * *

The smell of roasting meat drifts up to my room. We are to dine tonight with a Doctor and Madame Fortier. Scientific colleagues. I take a deep breath and inflate my lungs against the stays of my corset. My feelings towards the garment veer between love and hate; this evening they are definitely of the latter sort.

A knock at the door. Papa stands on the threshold, hair neatly combed away from his face with a slick of pomade. He is my father and he is not: seeing him properly and publicly at work has cast him in a subtly different light.

'Elise tells me dinner is almost ready. May I escort you?'

I laugh and curtsey to welcome him into the room. 'Will Monsieur Demenÿ be joining us?'

'No, no. Georges cannot be persuaded to leave the Station before nightfall.' He peers into the bulging surface of the wall mirror and fiddles with his collar. I stifle a giggle at the sight of his bearded chin, distorted to grotesque proportions. 'Did you enjoy yourself today?'

'Very much.'

'Good. We worked hard, didn't we? And we shall dine well, too. I hope you're not too tired for company?'

'I'm fine.'

'Good.' He pauses and looks about the room, trails a finger along the book of secrets and sits on the bed. 'Francesca— Cece. We—'

'Yes, Papa?'

'You cannot call me that here,' he says, meeting my eyes for the first time. 'In Paris, I am your uncle.'

'My uncle?'

'Uncle Étienne, if you prefer.'

I sit beside him but he evades my eyes, apparently intrigued by the floral design of the counterpane. 'I don't understand.' My voice sounds small and distant, as though it belongs to someone else.

'Then don't try.' He pats my lap briskly and goes to the door. 'Just when we're in formal company, you understand.'

Following him down the spiral stairs, I force myself to concentrate on where I place my feet. I feel the pressure of questions gathering in my brain, but cannot say quite what they are. The handrail is cold to the touch but I hold it fast. There's a small circle of white hair on the back of my father's head that I've never noticed before. It's the last thing I see before everything goes black.

* * *

After the fuss caused by my faint, the theories, the inescapable lie down, the delayed dinner and the adieus to my father's guests, at last I'm alone in my room. I lift the sash but the still night air does nothing to clear my mind. At dinner I could only sit there dumbly, unable to call my father anything at all, whilst my unease coalesced into questions I could not ask. Why was he ashamed of me? What had I done wrong? Who was I, if not my father's daughter? Then certain facts had begun to present themselves, a procession of unwanted memories: discussions about marriage, emancipation. Leola asking me why Mamma has a different name.

What to present. What to eliminate.

Tonight a different face stares back from the looking glass. I force my mouth to shape the word, *illegitimate*. I am a girl, I am Italian, I am twelve years old. And I am illegitimate. Not quite proper, or presentable. A fact that may be hidden from view but never altered.

I sit on the edge of the bed, trace the floral pattern that earlier held my father's gaze. The book of secrets lays open on the pillow. On the flyleaf in my small, cramped hand are written four miserable words.

I AM THE SECRET.

VICTORIA STEWART

The Starlight Rooms

Synopsis
In late-1940s Liverpool, the investigation of a fatal shooting at a cinema draws nightclub owners Alf, Harry and Johnny into a web of police corruption and leads them to confront the legacy of their shared past in wartime Europe.

The manager and assistant manager of the Coronet Cinema are shot and killed, apparently during the course of a robbery. Murphy, one of the suspects identified by the police, claims that he was at The Starlight Rooms nightclub on the night in question. The owners of the club, brothers Alf and Harry and their friend Johnny, are unable to provide an alibi for Murphy. Alf begins to suspect that Johnny may be influencing the police and steering them towards placing the blame on Murphy, but is unable to prove this. Murphy is charged with the murder, jointly with another man, McQuillan, whom he claims never to have met.

Elizabeth, a young solicitor, is on Murphy's defence team and tries to find evidence to support his case, but her hopes fade when McQuillan changes his plea to guilty. Meanwhile, Harry's girlfriend Janette believes that her friend Nelly and Nelly's petty criminal boyfriend Davison are being pressured by the police into supporting the prosecution, in order save themselves from prison. When Alf sees a picture of the Coronet's assistant manager, he recognises him from when he, Harry and Johnny were Special Operations Executive agents in France during the war. He realises that this man was the real target of the shooting, rather than it being part of a robbery gone wrong, and that Johnny has supported the tainted prosecution to protect himself and the real culprits. By the time Alf realises the truth, Murphy has been found guilty, but Alf persuades Johnny to provide evidence for an appeal.

The Starlight Rooms
When shots were fired in the manager's office at the Coronet Cinema, no one in the auditorium realised what had happened, not at first. With the music swelling as *The Bad Lord Byron* drew to a close, some thought that what they'd heard was the sound of seats tipping up as people stood to leave. But soon the occupants of the rows at the back of the stalls nearest to the foyer caught the sound of screams and doors slamming, and before

'The End' had quite appeared, the house lights were suddenly switched on and a woman called out from up in the balcony: 'Everybody stay sitting down please, no cause for alarm, please stay seated.' It didn't sound like the voice of someone who was used to being in charge, and when the customers sitting up there looked round, they saw that it was Ruby, one of the usherettes, and she was wide-eyed and distraught. Before anyone could ask her what had happened, she left again, and of course people didn't stay in their seats, they got up to see if they could discover what was going on. Those upstairs began to crowd onto the landing, and downstairs, they went out into the foyer. But the main doors leading to the pavement had been locked, and Mr Black, the Commissionaire, was standing in front of them, the keys still in his hand, looking as wild and confused as Ruby had. A murmur rose. 'What's going on, Mr Black? What's happening? Why can't we leave?' and he gulped for air and raised a hand to quieten them and said, 'I'm sorry, ladies and gents, we're going to have to wait for the police to arrive, they're on the way, there's been – there's been an incident.' And although he didn't mention anything about shots being fired or anyone being hurt, somehow, over the next few minutes, as people realised that they weren't going to be able to go home and drifted back inside, some of them standing talking in the aisles, others sitting down again resignedly, somehow, word began to leak out that there had been a robbery, that someone had been injured, a member of staff, not just injured, but shot, not just shot, but killed.

* * *

About a mile or so away, at The Starlight Rooms, Harry Bellamy saw his brother Alf give him a nod, and, as Alf began to play the opening chords of 'Prisoner of Love', the regulars moved away to the sides of the dance floor, and let Harry walk across to where Janette was leaning against the bar. She stepped into his arms, and to a ripple of respectful applause, they began to dance, the star shapes made by the covers clipped onto the spotlights scattering across Janette's dress as she moved. The first time they'd danced together to this song, some months previously, it had been spontaneous, a sudden whim on the part of Harry, who usually remained aloof from the frivolity, keeping an eye on the bar, ready to sort out any problems that might arise. He had offered Janette his hand, half expecting her to refuse, but she'd moved towards him and they'd set off together as though they'd rehearsed it, and other couples on the floor, recognising something special, or at least unusual, had made way for them. After that, without them ever discussing it, Harry and Janette's dance to 'Prisoner of Love' had become a regular feature as evenings at The Starlight Rooms

The Starlight Rooms

entered their final stages. A couple of weeks ago, someone had chucked a handful of peanuts across the floor as they turned and swayed: Janette stepped over them, giving no sign of having even noticed, and Harry had raised a murmur of laughter by kicking some of them out of the way with his heel and spinning her away from that corner without losing a beat. He'd been dimly aware of some scuffling, a door opening. Later he'd seen Johnny talking to Fred, the big barman who dealt with their occasional troublemakers, and when he approached them, Johnny had raised an eyebrow, gestured to the exit, and said, 'Hope that joker likes to take his food through a straw, that's what he'll be doing for a while.'

No trouble of that kind tonight: not often any trouble of any kind, with Johnny looking over the shoulder of the girl on the desk, refusing entry to anyone he didn't like the look of, and Harry making his presence known upstairs, a glance from him usually enough to halt an argument, or to give Billy permission to stop serving someone who'd had a skinful. He liked how it felt to hold Janette close to him, then to spin her away, then to draw her back. Their eyes rarely met, but when they did, he had a sense that maybe tonight would be one of the nights when, after the lights went up, instead of pulling her mink on over her silky red dress and disappearing off with a wriggle of her fingers in his general direction, she would stay and have a drink with him and Alf and Johnny and Billy and Fred and the band, and then follow him and Alf upstairs, and then follow him into his bedroom and let that dress slip off and climb under the covers with him. Thinking about that, he couldn't stop himself from giving her a wink, the merest flicker of his eyelid, as she passed from one hand to the other, and she raised an eyebrow just the least amount possible in response.

The next morning, he woke before she did, pulled on his trousers and went to the alcove that served as the kitchen, careful to try not to wake Alf as he passed through the room which was the nearest they had to a sitting room but was also where, behind a folding screen, Alf slept, or tried to sleep. He made a pot of tea, smoking a cigarette while the kettle was boiling. When he brought the two cups back into the bedroom, Janette was awake, propping herself on a pillow, the covers pulled up to her chin more for warmth than modesty. He went round the bed and she moved over a little so that he could sit on the edge of the mattress next to her. He handed her her cup and saucer. There were no bedside tables, just the bed, a wardrobe, a chest of drawers with his brushes and cuff-links scattered on top, and a straight-backed chair heaped with last night's clothes. From the other room, came the sound of Alf coughing; maybe he'd already been awake after all. Janette sipped her tea.

'Thank you, darling.' She sipped again, and then said, 'He needs to get that seen to.'

'It's always bad in the mornings. They can't do much more than they've done already. Cold weather doesn't help. He prefers it damp.'

'You came to the right place for that.'

'We did.'

They drank. He looked at her, thinking about how he'd like to push the sheet down and put his hands, his tongue, on her breasts. Let her finish her tea first. From how she looked at him, he guessed that she wouldn't say no to another go around. She said, 'I was talking to a nice girl last night, girl he might like, quiet one, red-head – would that cheer him up?'

She'd made suggestions of this sort before, never insistently.

'I don't think so, love.'

She shrugged, let it pass.

'She didn't believe you were brothers, this girl, you're so unalike.'

'Yeah, well I got the looks, didn't I?' he said, puffing his chest out, but laughing at himself. Then he said, 'When we had the act, before the war, we were called The Twins, Les Jumeaux it is in French. It was a kind of joke, because we don't look anything like.'

She smiled. Johnny still called him and Alf 'The Twins' sometimes, and she must have wondered what that was all about, but she never asked about the war or before the war, and he liked her for it. He didn't know what she knew, but Johnny never lost the opportunity to spin a line. She probably thought all sorts. He liked how she looked when her make-up had worn off, the contrast it made with the gloss and powder of the night before. It was hard to believe that she'd be able to fix that big black cloud of hair into its usual neat arrangement, pulled tight against her scalp and twisted into a hard knot at the back of her head. He finished his tea and put the cup and saucer down, and watched her as she finished hers. He wished there'd been a biscuit left to give her.

'But Alf must be older than you?'

'No, me, I'm eight years older than him.'

'Never!' She couldn't hide her surprise. Then she must have realised that if it was flattering to him, it also spoke volumes about his brother, because she glanced in the direction of his increasingly persistent coughing and said, 'Poor old Alf.' She gave Harry her cup and saucer, and he put in on the floor with his own, and then leaned over her, kissed her, slipped a hand down under the sheet, murmuring, 'He'll be all right. He's tough as old boots. Don't worry about him.'

Eventually, they got up and Janette slid back into her dress, put her face on and did what she could to put her hair in order. When they went through to the other room, Alf had folded his bed and the screen away into their corner and was sitting at the table, smoking. He must have been out, because he was reading the *Post*. From this angle, Harry noticed, the hair on Alf's neck, where it was cut short, looked very grey. He hadn't had a shave yet, and his beard was silvery as well. He looked tired, but then, he usually looked tired, or in pain, or a combination of both. Harry said to Janette, 'Do you want some breakfast before you go, love? Got some eggs there.'

'No, I'll leave you to it, that cup of tea set me up, thanks for that.'

Not raising his eyes to them, Alf said, 'Cup of tea? I'll have one if there's one going.'

'What did your last servant die of?' said Harry. 'I'll just let Janette out and I'll put the kettle on.'

'Here.' Alf lifted the newspaper and picked up the keys from the table. As Harry approached to take them out of his hand, he gestured to the paper.

'What's new?' he said.

Alf folded the paper closed and showed him the headline on the front page: TWO DEAD IN SHOOTING AT CINEMA.

Janette must have seen it too, because she said, 'Whereabouts was it? Round here?'

'Not far,' said Alf. 'The Coronet, you know it?'

'Know of it. Not sure I've ever been there.' Harry took the paper and glanced over the piece. It had happened late last night, and there wasn't a lot of detail. 'Manager and one of the staff killed.'

'Why would you do a thing like that?' said Janette.

'For the takings, suppose.'

'How much takings would a cinema have?'

'It doesn't say,' said Harry, putting the paper back on the table. 'Not enough to risk swinging for it, I wouldn't have thought.'

'You ever worry about something like that happening here?' said Janette, settling her coat onto her shoulders. Her eyes were wide and she seemed bothered by this shooting, though it was hardly next door, and hardly the sort of thing that happened every weekend. Harry went towards her, ran his hand down her arm.

'Nothing like that'll be happening here. Can you imagine Johnny letting anything like that happen?' That made her smile a little. She moved away from him and picked her handbag up, and as she rifled through it, she said, 'Well, I'll see you tonight then?' to Alf, and he said, 'Sure, darling, see you later.'

Harry let her go down the stairs in front of him, watching her as she picked her way on the narrow treads, holding onto the rail, placing each foot carefully. When they got to the bottom, he unlocked the street door, and before he opened it, while they were standing there in the narrow space behind it, he said, quietly, 'You want me to get you a taxi, love?'

'No, darling, it's not far.'

He didn't know where she lived; he'd never asked and she'd never said. He didn't much like the idea of her going out into the street still dressed up from the night before. Sometimes she arrived for work in ordinary clothes, with her evening dress and shoes in a bag; he supposed it depended on what she'd been doing beforehand, but he'd never asked her about that either. In any case, she didn't seem to care what people might think. She kissed him on the cheek and patted him on the arm, and squeezed up against him so that there was room for the door to open, and he took the opportunity to run his hand over her bottom, pull her towards him, bury his nose into the silky collar of her coat, making her wriggle as he breathed against her neck, but she was having none of it, slapped his hand away and stepped outside into the day. She didn't look back and he wasn't wearing any shoes so didn't follow her out into the alleyway. It smelt bad out there this morning; he closed the door and went back upstairs.

Alf hadn't moved. Harry went and put the kettle on, then went back in and took a cigarette from the packet on the table.

'You all right?' he said to Alf.

'Much as ever.' He turned a page, and then said, 'She's a nice girl, Janette.'

It was the closest he'd ever come to alluding to the fact that she sometimes stayed the night there, but then he didn't say much about anything these days. Of course it was difficult to get a word in sideways when Johnny was around, as he so often was.

'I like her,' said Harry. And then, because he felt he ought to, he added, 'Nothing serious, mind.'

Alf gave a shrug, as though it made no difference to him, turned another page, and then folded the paper back on itself so that the list of runners in the afternoon's races at Aintree was visible, and offered it to Harry. 'While you're making that tea, see if you fancy any of these for a few bob.'

BEN SUMMERS

Looking for Romance (with Steve Davis)
A story of Northern Soul Down South

Synopsis
Romance is on a quest: to explore the wonders of soul music – and thereby the meaning of life – through his art. He wants to make a documentary about looking for his soul idol, Romance Watson, and he wants snooker player and fellow soul-lover Steve Davis to be involved. But Romance's love life and the eccentric escapades of his soul friends serve to confuse more than enlighten.

As Romance works on his fanciful film ideas, Spaghetti Weston grieves for his dead soul dog and Demetrius Demetriou dies of cancer, taking some of his records to his grave, including, Romance believes, a rare pressing of a Romance Watson. Meanwhile, an intelligently depressed vagrant, Hippy John, is talked out of suicide by Lee, a brash soul builder.

Spaghetti feels a religious calling and there's a gentle exchange of understanding between the soul folk and the troubled, philosophically minded Hippy John. A northern soul vicar, who found both God and soul music after a bump on the head, embraces the holy trinity that is God, love and rare soul music.

Romance's quest appears as dependent upon loneliness and heartbreak as soul music itself, but then a cheery new love enters his life. Surprisingly, Romance receives some personal advice from Romance Watson himself – that love itself is the greatest testament to the greatness of soul.

At a soul do to commemorate the life of Demetrius Demetriou, Spaghetti and Hippy John witness an impromptu ceremony, officiated by the soul vicar, to solidify the bond between Romance and his cheery new companion. The loving spirit of Demetrius Demetriou is pleased and the Godly, timeless, spaceless force of music is duly honoured.

1
'Soul Sam is dead!'

Romance didn't know what to say. Another soul death. There was no reason for him not to believe it. It was one of those occasions on which he knew he should say something and it was one of those occasions on which he knew he should feel something, but he didn't say anything and the main thing he felt was a dizzying mix of guilt and confusion for not feeling more. Soul Sam was his hero.

'He had a stroke. He died in the night.'

Immediately, ashamedly, Romance was aware that he resented his friend for having this inside knowledge. But he liked Spaghetti. He loved him.

'I ain't sure I'm gonna be able to make it Saturday, mate.'

Now Romance was overflowing with feeling and it was a feeling like some Brummie twit had just turned off the turnable midway through a record and time had resoundingly crashed to a halt. This was terrible news. Spaghetti was supposed to be DJing on Saturday. Of course, Soul Sam's death was terrible news too, especially for Soul Sam, but surely Saturday could still be Saturday. And Saturday mattered. Saturday was the memorial do for Demetrios.

Immediately, ashamedly, Romance found himself more worried about Saturday than he was worried by the thought of a world without Soul Sam. And he loved Soul Sam. Soul Sam was his hero. But a world without Soul Sam was a long-term proposition; it had only just started. Saturday was on Saturday. And it was for his friend.

'I know it weren't totally unexpected like, but it's knocked me for six a bit, mate. We're gonna bury him in the garden.'

At that, Romance just waited. When someone said something so disorienting – like when Catford Keith told him that he (Catford Keith) was growing younger every year because his old cells were continually being replaced by new ones – he reckoned he just had to wait until they said something he could say something back to. And what did Spaghetti mean it wasn't totally unexpected? Romance hadn't even known Soul Sam was sick. Did everyone know but him?

Romance was familiar with the garden. It was at the back of Spaghetti's semi in Birmingham, where he lived with Annie. There was a square of grass and a washing line and wooden fences around, and beyond the fences were the gardens of other Birmingham semis. It didn't seem fitting as the final resting place of the world's leading cultural icon. Surely there was somewhere with a little more gravitas – a gravesite with a little more soul. Somewhere in Cleethorpes. Or Great Yarmouth, maybe. Or Detroit.

And, if it was to be a garden, Romance's was better anyway. It was longer and more coffin-shaped. It wasn't Detroit or Chicago, but surely the London Borough of Brent had as much soul as Birmingham?

'Annie says it's barmy, but I think it's what he would have wanted. I've had him ever since he was a babby.'

A babby. Since he was a babby.

'You stupid fucking Brummie twat,' Romance thought but didn't say.

(What he said was 'Oh, I'm really sorry.') The stupid fucking Brummie twat was talking about his stupid fucking Brummie dog.

Romance knew that Spaghetti loved his dog more than was normal even for a dog lover, and because Spaghetti loved his dog so much Romance loved Spaghetti even more than he would have done anyway, which would have been a lot. And Romance could hear that Spaghetti was upset.

'Sorry about Saturday mate, but I just don't think I'll be in the mood.'

'Don't worry, Spag-man. Just come down if you feel like it on the day,' Romance said, hopefully, and he thought, bitterly, about being blown out because of a fucking dog: an ugly, old, crippled Brummie dog that had been blind in one eye and had lost control of its bladder. But Romance loved Spaghetti, and he loved Spaghetti loving his dog, and he loved that he had called his dog after Soul Sam. And, when he thought about it (which was after the phone call but before *Countdown*), he came to the conclusion that the kind of DJ he wanted DJing at the memorial do for Demetrios Demetriou was just the kind of DJ who would cancel because his dog had died. And so he was pleased with himself for asking Spaghetti in the first place. The whole episode had simply confirmed his excellent judgement.

2

Sam Cooke was the original Soul Sam, although he was never known as Soul Sam and neither the human nor the canine Soul Sam to follow was named after him. But he was one of soul music's originators and there has never been another Sam in soul music to rival him. He was the first well-known singer to make the move from church to rhythm and blues... and to soul. And he was one of the first to die.

The official Los Angeles Police Department record states that Cooke was shot and killed by Bertha Franklin, the manager of the Hacienda Motel. Cooke had checked into the motel one evening and Franklin claimed that in the night he broke into her live-in office in a rage, wearing nothing but a shoe and an overcoat, demanding to know the whereabouts of a young woman who had accompanied him to the motel. Franklin denied any knowledge of the woman, but the enraged Cooke didn't believe her and violently grabbed her. According to Franklin, she grappled with Cooke, the two of them fell to the floor and then she jumped up and ran to get her gun. She said that she fired at Cooke in self-defence because she feared for her life. She shot three times. Cooke exclaimed, 'Lady, you shot me,' before falling, mortally wounded.

According to Franklin and the motel's owner, Evelyn Carr, they were on the phone together at the time of the incident. Cooke interrupted them and then Franklin dropped the phone in the struggle, but her boss continued to listen. Carr then called the police, saying that she thought there had been a shooting. 'A guy just broke through the door... I think she shot him, I don't know.'

Whenever Spaghetti heard the Sam Cooke song *You Send Me* (which was as little as possible as he considered it a sorry example of the pop schmaltz that Cooke fell into), he heard the words 'Lady, you shot me' in place of 'Darling, you send me'. And he wondered at the coincidence of the two female protagonists, Bertha Franklin and Evelyn Carr, sharing surnames with two of the greatest soul voices of all time: Aretha Franklin and James Carr. The world of soul music leaves many unanswered questions. But that's what it is to be human, Spaghetti concluded (even though the Franklin/Carr coincidence was clearly just a coincidence and not a particularly remarkable one at that).

3

Soul Sam's funeral was a sombre affair. Spaghetti oversaw proceedings and Annie attended. Spaghetti had managed to squeeze Soul Sam into a record carrying case before he had gone too stiff and it made a good coffin and was a loving touch because Spaghetti loved his records. He loved his records and he loved his dog. (And he loved Annie, but that was a different kind of love.) He *had* loved his dog. Now his dog was gone. He still had his records. And he had Annie.

'So what records were in that box?' little Annie asked when she saw Soul Sam during the wake.

'Just some old reissues. Nothing special.'

'And where are they gonna go now? You're not having any down here you know.'

The records had a habit of creeping down and Annie was always on her guard. Spaghetti had a record room, but it wasn't big enough.

'They're just on the floor of the record room. Don't make such a fuss.'

Annie suspected that Spaghetti was planning on taking advantage of the death of Soul Sam by sneaking some records down, thinking that concern and sympathy for his loss would stop her from intervening. The sight of Soul Sam in the open record box heightened her suspicion. But Spaghetti would never have taken advantage of the death of Soul Sam in that or any other way, and that was just one of the reasons Romance had wanted him to DJ at the memorial do for Demetrios Demetriou. The man had soul.

'That dog had soul,' said Spaghetti to himself, as Annie tried to wrestle Soul Sam from the box. But he was stiff now and had jammed fast.

Romance had met Soul Sam a few times – on his only visit to Spaghetti's house, when Soul Sam had lain dutifully on the landing as Romance and Spaghetti had sat in Spaghetti's record room playing Billy Stewart flipsides, and, of course, at various soul dos – but he hadn't known the dog was called Soul Sam. When talking to the dog, Spaghetti simply called him 'mate' or 'Sammy boy'. But the funeral was a formal affair and Spaghetti felt it right and proper that Soul Sam be called by his right and proper name.

'Soul Sam was so beautiful, like flowers full bloom in May. His kiss was like the summer breeze; it left me speechless, with nothing left to say. I loved and I lost. It happens to the best. I loved and I lost. I might as well confess.'

When spoken by a mourning Brummie at a dog's funeral, it isn't immediately obvious that those are the lyrics of a classic Impressions song (with the little addition of a new name and a subtle switch of gender). But even Annie was moved.

'That was beautiful. Poor Soul Sam.'

'Curtis Mayfield, init. He must have gone through what I'm going through now.'

And for Romance and Spaghetti that was the beauty of the music. When their hearts were broken and they felt as if they were broken as no hearts had ever been broken before, it reached out to them and showed them that others had been there, that it was a part of being human and that they were among many and a part of the whole. And because they were a part of the whole, they still had a place in the world. And it didn't just tell them as pop music did; it showed them. The pain resonated through the music.

Spaghetti had dug a hole in the grass about two and a half 45s wide, a couple deep and about a 150 (upright) long. He picked up the record box containing Soul Sam and lowered it in. He threw a handful of earth on top of it.

'Ashes to ashes, dust to dust... How does it go, bab?'

Annie shrugged.

'Ashes to ashes, dust to dust, here lies Soul Sam, in dog we trust.'

'What does that mean, *in dog we trust*?'

'I'm not sure. It just came out.'

Spaghetti was the officiator. Annie was a mourner. They hadn't invited anyone else to the funeral. They had thought about it, but Soul Sam didn't really have any close dog friends as he didn't get out much and few humans seemed appropriate, other than the human Soul Sam. Spaghetti had asked him, but, once the human Soul Sam realised that the voice on the phone belonged to Spaghetti Weston and wasn't that of a Brummie St. Peter informing him of his own demise, he decided to say that he was already booked on that afternoon to DJ at a donkey wedding in Blackpool. He had never DJed at a dog's funeral and wouldn't know what to play, and he wasn't able to grasp that he didn't have to play anything because, in the twenty-five years since he first stepped up before the soul masses of the Wigan Casino, no one had ever asked him anywhere to do anything other than play records.

Spaghetti was wearing his dressing gown. He had told Annie that he thought the priestly effect befitted the occasion. He was trying to keep a candle alight too, but the wind kept blowing it out.

'Does *Ashes to Ashes* mean you should burn him? Shouldn't we have a dog cremation?' Annie suggested, as Spaghetti was already covering the record box with earth.

'Burn Soul Sam? I don't want to burn Soul Sam. I want to give him a grave and a headstone.'

'A headstone? You never said anything about a headstone! I don't know if I want a headstone in the middle of the lawn.'

'He's gotta have a headstone, bab. How can you bury him and not give him a headstone? I'm going to make it out of vinyl and put an inscription on it from one of his favourite records.'

'Well as long as it's not *In Dog We Trust*.' Annie shook her head but wasn't going to press the matter.

'It wasn't going to be *In Dog We Trust*,' Spaghetti muttered to himself as he kept filling the hole, although he did think that had a nice ring to it. He didn't yet know what it was going to be, but it had to be something because Sammy boy needed a memorial and anyway the record box was metal and how could he burn that? Even if he were able to produce enough heat, which he wouldn't be, the box would just melt and form a globby mass of metallic dog, which they would then just have to bury anyway, and that wouldn't be a fitting end to a dog of Soul Sam's stature.

'Here lies Soul Sam, the most soulful dog in Birming-ham.' Spaghetti would have to think about it.

Unlike Soul Sam, Sam Cooke had two funerals and, unlike Soul Sam's, both were national events. He drew the biggest crowds of his career.

In Los Angeles, for three days Sam's body was held in state in an open casket. It was then taken to Chicago for one funeral service and then back to Los Angeles for another. Two other soul luminaries, Lou Rawls and Bobby Bland, were among those who sang at the LA funeral. Strangely, Sam was dressed differently for the two funerals and, even more strangely, in LA his coffin was presented standing upright. 'Until the day break and the shadows flee away,' reads his headstone. 'I will get me to the mountain of myrrh and the hill of frankincense,' continues the Song of Solomon. It's all about the meaning of true love. It's all about soul.

Biographies

Judge

Naomi Wood is the author of *The Godless Boys* (Picador, 2011) and the award-winning *Mrs. Hemingway* (Picador, 2014) which won the British Library Writers Award, the Jerwood Fiction Uncovered Award, was shortlisted for the International Dylan Thomas Award, and was a Richard and Judy book-club choice. *The Hiding Game*, Naomi's third novel, was published in 2019 by Picador. Set in the Bauhaus art school in the centenery of its founding, it has been described as 'a great gift' (*Irish Times*); 'propulsive' (*Guardian*) and 'devastating' (*New Statesman*). Naomi's work is available in sixteen languages. She teaches at UEA and lives in Norwich with her family.

Daniel Allen is a freelance journalist with long experience of writing for magazines, newspapers and websites. He completed a master's degree in creative writing at Bath Spa University in 2015 and has written short stories, poetry, a play and an unpublished novel. He was runner-up in the 2018 Brighton Prize flash fiction category and is a member of a local writing group. He has performed stand-up comedy at the Edinburgh Fringe and at numerous comedy clubs, and has written sketches for the Brighton-based Treason Show, a satirical news review.

Rebecca Blakkr is a Creative Director and writer based in London and Cambridge. Her conceptual artworks have been commissioned by institutions such as the Barbican. She took a radical break from her career to become a boxing promoter, though it came to an abrupt end when someone took exception to her liberal views. Her luck almost ran out again when she became tangled in a parachute at 5,000 feet, but back on earth she subsequently vowed to get on with her first novel. She is a graduate of Curtis Brown Creative and has previously been shortlisted for The British Short Screenplay Competition.
Instagram: @blakkr_   Twitter: @blakkr_

Hannah Colby graduated from the University Of York with a 2:1 in English Literature & Politics and works as a freelance writer in her home town of Norwich. She's a columnist for several local publications and has just completed her novel, *The Invisible World*. Hannah's genre is historical fiction, which comes as no surprise to anyone who knows her; she's passionate about vintage music and swing dancing and when she's not writing, she can be found running Lindy Hop classes and events.

Órla Cronin is a writer, research psychologist and sailor. She particularly loves high latitude sailing, and has staffed sailing expeditions in Antarctica and the Arctic. *Brash and Frazil* is her first novel, started during a glorious two years doing an MA at the Centre for New Writing, University of Manchester. An additional extract from *Brash and Frazil* can be seen in the Manchester Anthology VI https://themanchesteranthologyvi.blogspot.com/ Other publications and awards include shortlisted flash fiction in the Chorlton Arts Festival, and a much cherished prize for the 'best opening line' at the Bath Flash Fiction Festival.

Kitty Edwards grew up in Manchester, the daughter of a botanist and a South African Indian immigrant. She travelled widely with her parents and, later in life, independently. She studied law at Oxford and practiced in London for several years. She now lives in Hertfordshire with her husband, two young daughters and a cat. Outside writing, her hobbies include cycling, gardening and supporting SEN children. *The Alchemy of Botany* is her first novel.

Leonora Gale grew up on the west coast of Wales, in Pembrokeshire. She studied Literature at Goldsmith's, University of London, before returning home to spend twelve years following the head rather than the heart, running her own hospitality businesses. Her day-to-day life running a Michelin listed hotel and restaurant was featured in a 2012 BBC Wales documentary, *A Summer in Wales*. Since leaving behind the demands of running a hotel in 2017, she has finally been able to finally follow the heart, and spend time writing. She is currently working on her second novel, a contemporary retelling of *Dracula*.

Mel Gough was born in Germany and now lives in London. Her self-published romantic suspense novel *He is Mine* was shortlisted for the 2019 Bookbrunch Selfies Awards. One of her short stories has appeared in the Fluky Fiction Valentine's Day anthology.

Sean Gregory has been, amongst other things, a musician and award-winning theatre maker. He won a Skillset bursary to study on the Creative Writing MA at University of East Anglia. In 2019, he completed his PhD at University of Salford, a creative and critical thesis on the life and work of Anthony Burgess. He has been the recipient of a Peggy Ramsay Bursary and was briefly in John Cooper Clarke's backing band. Sean grew up Manchester and lives in West Yorkshire. He is currently working on his second novel.

Aisha Hassan recently completed a Masters in Creative Writing at the University of Oxford. She was shortlisted for the Poetry School / Nine Arches Press Primers competition 2017. Her play *Pickled Mangoes* was performed at the Tamasha comedy scratch night performance at Soho Theatre in June 2017. Her work has appeared in *Under the Radar* and *Campus* magazines. She lives and works in London and wishes she had a dog called Bojo.

Christopher Holt was born in Exeter but has lived in Africa and Australia and, for a short time, in East Germany (DDR). He has worked as a teacher, ecologist, administrator and broadcaster and has a life-long interest in the natural environment. *The Good Steward* is Christopher's fifth novel. Three of his other four books, all self-published, were awarded the American *Book Readers' Association Medallion*. His fourth novel, *Orphaned Leaves,* won the Yeovil Literary Prize in 2016 and came second in the Bridport Prize the same year. It was also in the final of the Exeter Novel Prize in 2015.

Emily Hughes is a teacher and has studied photography, literature and foreign languages. She started writing *Ghost Boy* after working with young people with special needs, and following her own son's diagnosis of autism; after attending an Arvon writing course, she was encouraged to continue with her story. Emily blogs about photography and creative writing and is particularly interested in exploring the themes of family, relationships, identity and memory. Emily can usually be found with a camera in hand or at her laptop, writing, often burning her children's dinner. Emily was also recently long listed for the Bath First Novel Award.

Sandra Jensen was born in South Africa and has British and Canadian citizenship. Her work has appeared in *World Literature Today*, *The Irish Times*, *Wasafiri*, *AGNI* and *Flash: The International Short-Short Story Magazine*, among others. Her awards include winning the *bosque* Fiction Prize, the J.G. Farrell award for best novel-in-progress and Highly Commended for the 2012 Bridport Prize short story competition. Sandra was a guest writer and panellist at the 12th, 13th and 15th International Conference on the Short Story in English and taught writing workshops at The Galle Literary Festival, Sri Lanka and for the British Council in Colombo.

George Kelly is a writer, teacher, entrepreneur, and a former battle rapper. His short stories have been published in *The Literary Hatchet* and *Ink Stains*, and he's worked on numerous film scripts with UK feature film director Regan Hall (*Fast Girls*). In his battle rap days he toured England and performed in front of thousands of drunk fans. He also battled at *Outlook Festival* in Croatia and on Venice Beach. He's the founder of *The Write Path*, an award-winning creative writing course designed to help at-risk teens express themselves and re-engage with education. He's married to the love of his life and has four beautiful kids.

Wenyan Lu is a native of Shanghai, who moved to the UK in 2006. She teaches English and Chinese, and translates literary non-fiction including poetry. She is the Chinese translator of Robert Macfarlane's *Mountains of the Mind*. Wenyan holds a Master of Studies in Creative Writing from the University of Cambridge. She was longlisted for the SI Leeds Literary Prize in 2018. When she is not writing, Wenyan loves cooking and calligraphy. She lives in Cambridge with her family.

John O'Donnell was born in London's east end to Irish parents. He left school early in search of an education. A variety of jobs followed. Most notably, a spell at Watford Palace Theatre as an assistant stage manager, and ten years in the advertising business as a copywriter. He quit to become a proper writer. He has written for film, an adaption of John B Keane's *Durango*, and for television: 'The Bill', 'Heartbeat', 'Where the Heart Is'. *The Only Life You Could Save* is his first novel.

Sophie O'Mahony began her career in journalism, before deciding to pursue a career in law. She now works as a solicitor in London. She writes in her spare time and has produced a collection of short stories and plays and is currently developing a TV pilot script. *Third Space* is her first novel.

Sarah Reynolds is originally from Surrey and has lived in Wales for ten years. She learnt Welsh fluently and has written two novellas for Welsh learners: *Dysgu Byw* and *Cyffesion Saesnes yng Nghymru*. Her short stories and articles have been featured in publications including *Wales*

Arts Review, *O'r Pedwar Gwyn*t and *New Welsh Review*. In 2014 Sarah won the Rhys Davies Short Story Prize; the story was later adapted into a BAFTA Cymru-winning short film: *Helfa'r Heli (Catch of the Day)*. Sarah has recently completed a PhD in Creative Writing at Aberystwyth University. *The Haven* is her first full-length novel.

Sally Skinner was born in Derbyshire in 1981 and read English at Girton College, Cambridge. After several years working as a copywriter and ad creative, she gained a Distinction on the Creative Writing Masters at Royal Holloway. She lives in East London with her husband and two daughters.

Victoria Stewart grew up near Liverpool. Her fiction has been longlisted for the Lucy Cavendish Fiction Prize (2017) and shortlisted for the Richard and Judy Search for a Bestseller Competition (2018). She teaches English Literature at the University of Leicester and has published academic books and articles on war writing and crime writing, including *Crime Writing in Interwar Britain: Fact and Fiction in the Golden Age* (Cambridge University Press, 2017). Victoria is on twitter @verbivorial

Ben Summers is a politics graduate from London and has worked for nearly thirty years as a television producer and director. In 2006, his documentary 'Baghdad: A Doctor's Story' won an international Emmy award. For other films he has won a Most Creative Documentary award, an Excellence in Media award and has been nominated for a BAFTA. *The Guardian* has published articles relating to his work. He's an enthusiastic collector of rare soul 45s, has DJ'd extensively on the Northern Soul scene and has his own record sales website. He lives in Somerset with his girlfriend, Catherine, and Bella the poodle.